ACCIDENT

Katherine Jones
(née Scourse)

First Impression—2002

ISBN 1 84323 183 2

This book is published with the support of the Arts Council of Wales.

Printed in Wales at
Gomer Press, Llandysul, Ceredigion

To the memory of my parents,
Phyllis and Reginald Scourse,
who died too young

The author, with her husband on his first day out of hospital

Kath, Gareth, with son, Matthew, and daughter, Bethan

Foreword

Sometimes, in the darkest hours of the months following my husband's road accident, one or other of our family would say 'people should know what it's like. Nobody has any idea of what we're going through unless they've faced such a disaster themselves.' Ten years later, I feel this even more strongly and so have decided to make public the series of horrors and successes which made up his five months of hospitalisation. In this period Gareth was brought from death's door to a stable condition in which he could survive as a tetraplegic, paralysed from the chest down. I sincerely hope that reading about these experiences will be useful not only for those patients and their families embarking on this particular painful journey but for everybody who has any experience of hospitals.

I wanted also to show in detail what such a life involves; the living on a knife edge, the constant struggle against further disaster. So, apart from the narrative sequence of nine chapters describing everything from the car crash to Gareth's coming out of hospital, I include eight interludes designed to show the difference between life before and after the accident – contrasting various holidays, journeys and levels of independence – culminating in the last interlude 'The Same and not the Same'. Should this go some way towards furthering an understanding of disabled people and modify commonly-found attitudes of patronising kindness or simple dismissal I would be more than happy.

During my husband's time in hospital I kept a brief factual diary of events. Our daughter Bethan kept a much longer and more emotional daily account. These, together with memories neither Gareth nor Matthew, our son, will ever be able to forget, form the basis of my truthful account of all that happened. I am especially grateful to all the staff of Gomer Press, particularly my editors Francesca Rhydderch and Ceri Wyn Jones, for ensuring that the story will reach a wider audience.

After much thought I decided it was expedient for all participants in this drama (apart from the family) to be given pseudonyms, although there are some people who will be able to recognize themselves and others. Nevertheless I must identify here a few people who played crucial roles in Gareth's struggles. Dr Wise, one of the consultants in the intensive care unit of Cardiff Royal Infirmary was well nigh perfect in his concern for the quality of patients' lives extending well beyond the physical, his understanding of the needs of families and his innovative use of resources to suit specific cases. (His death shortly after retirement remains a source of the profoundest regret). Mr Ceri Hoddinott showed us the human face of high-ranking medical staff. Medically founded or not, we are all convinced that Dr Moira Evans was instrumental in saving Gareth's life at one stage of his treatment. At Rookwood Hospital, Dr Alison Grant masterminded Gareth's rehabilitation with a wonderful mixture of expertise, authority and sympathy. Mrs Wei Lee, at the time our local community nurse team leader, was inspirational.

In some ways it is invidious to single out even these remarkable people. So many hospital nurses, doctors, occupational therapists (in particular another Cath Jones – and Alan, her technician who meticulously made with skill and patience the aids prescribed for those in need), physiotherapists (especially 'John' in the narrative whose real name I cannot trace), the encouraging Cardiff Royal Infirmary porters and, since Gareth's return home, GPs and community nurses (notably Louise Fritche) have played a crucial role in recovery and rehabilitation.

How can I begin to express our gratitude to the vast array of friends, family and professional colleagues who wrote, telephoned, sent gifts and visited not only throughout a long period in hospital but, in some cases, right up to the present day? By their concern and practical help they have bolstered morale, even the will to survive. My sisters and their husbands lent most active support throughout the worst times and ever since have been largely instrumental in helping us develop a surprisingly full and active life.

As for Bethan and Matthew, our daughter and son, no words can describe what they meant to us during that time and in the ten years which have since elapsed. I can only wish that others facing similar disasters have the help of such people whose love and vibrant personalities can make terrible events the means of strengthening family ties.

1

Disaster

It was a hot day. A long, dry spell had just been broken by a sudden shower. Two cars approached each other near Golden Grove on the road between Llandeilo and Cross Hands in Carmarthenshire. It was quite a narrow stretch and there were several bends in quick succession. One of the two cars climbed slowly up hill. The other rounded a corner at speed, lost control and hurtled across the road directly into the path of the oncoming car, a mere yard in front of it. There was nowhere for the slower driver to go, and no time to take evasive action, except to stamp on the brake with all his strength. There was a mighty impact. The empty passenger side of the speeding car hit the driver's side of the other with its full force. Here we have one more incident to add to road accident statistics. Here too we have innocent lives being irrevocably changed.

* * *

I wonder what we would have done had we known that this was the last day of our old life. It is probably just as well that we didn't know; imagine the impossibility of deciding what to do for the very last time and how to get the maximum intensity out of quite ordinary things that could never be the same again.

We had as much reason as anyone to live our lives thinking that disasters only happened to other people, and I think it can be truthfully said that none of our family had any serious forebodings about the future. No one could have been happier than we were about the characters and abilities of their children, and had looked forward to watching and helping them as their lives unfolded. My teaching post would become full-time so there would be no serious financial problems in having two children in university at the same time. Gareth, now a professor, had every reason to be pleased with the development of his career. Later on we would be able to devote our income to doing all those things – particularly extensive travelling – that we had put aside until such self-indulgence was feasible. Certain decisions had to be made before long, but there was no doubt about it; we were lucky.

There had been nothing unusual about Friday, 3 July 1992; it was just another ordinary day. After a day at school I had cooked tea for Matthew which he was eating in front of the television. Bethan had left that afternoon for a twenty-first birthday celebratory weekend in Birmingham. She'd gone in a rush without leaving the address and telephone number of the friend with whom she would be staying. Instead, pandering as usual to an over-anxious mother, she would ring when she arrived. I put a quiche in the oven so we could have a speedy tea as soon as Gareth came home. He and I were going to the opera that evening. Normally it was difficult to predict when both of us would be free, but for once we had ignored the possibility of a wasted expensive ticket and I was mildly exhilarated as I hurried upstairs to change. At that moment the phone rang and I answered cheerfully, only briefly thinking that it was probably Gareth warning me that he would be arriving at the last minute. An unknown voice asked if I was the wife of Gareth Jones. When I confirmed that I was, he said that Gareth had asked him to tell me that he would be delayed. This seemed odd since he could easily have asked his secretary to phone me. The stranger said he had been involved in a road accident with Gareth Jones.

'Is he alright?'

'We've left him in the car for now.'

I knew that after an accident nothing would have kept Gareth in the car but serious injury. He would normally have leapt out to examine the damage to his much-loved Honda and to exchange words with that other driver.

'How serious was the accident? You seem to be alright. It can't have been too bad, can it?'

'It was a hard collision . . . He just asked me to tell you he would be late.'

'We were going to the opera . . .'

'Oh, God. I'm sorry,' said the voice, sounding as if its owner had suddenly realised the magnitude of what he had done.

'But is he alright?' I persisted.

Again the guarded 'We've left him in the car for now.'

Suddenly he was gone and immediately I knew I had failed to ask the second most important question: 'Where is Gareth?' Trembling, I sat down by the phone and tried to convince myself that it was only a slight impact and that Gareth would be fine, if shaken. After all he had given the other driver our phone number and the message was only that he'd be late. But why had Gareth stayed in the car? Deep down I was certain that something was seriously wrong. What should I do? Cursing my stupidity in not asking where they were, I prepared for instant flight. I didn't tell Matthew what had happened: there was no point in worrying him unnecessarily. I removed the quiche from the oven – it wasn't even warm – and put my purse and keys near the door. Then I sat down again by the telephone.

About fifteen minutes after the first ring there was a second. Grabbing the receiver I recognised the voice of James, the husband of Margaret, who had been at the same meeting as Gareth in Aberystwyth. They had left shortly after him and were following the same route. He had nearly accepted an offer of a lift with them and had only refused because he thought that it might make us late for the opera. They had rounded a corner on the road to Cross Hands and, seeing an accident with police in attendance, had idly wondered what had happened. Something made one of them glance back and, only as they reached the next corner, recognised the crumpled car. They stopped at once and ran back along the road to the crash. Margaret got into the front passenger seat with Gareth and talked to him until the fire brigade and ambulance arrived.

It was impossible for Gareth to be lifted clear of the tangled wreckage without moving what could be a broken spine, so the firemen used powerful equipment to cut away the side pillar which separated the front door from the back. By this time the ambulance men had assessed his immediate needs, fitted him with a stiff neck collar and, by reclining the front seat, were able to ease him gently onto a stretcher. This was lifted into the ambulance and they started the fifteen mile journey to Glangwili hospital, leaving Gareth's pride and joy a 'write-off' in the hands of the police.

James and Margaret had been horrified witnesses of all this, but obviously only gave me the barest of necessary information in their phone call. James said Gareth was perfectly lucid and was speaking normally, but needed to be taken to hospital to be checked for injuries. He gave me clear directions to the hospital and told me that he and Margaret would be waiting for me in the car park.

At least the impotent waiting was over. In a few minutes I'd told Matthew what had happened and we were in the car. I tried to appear cheerful and matter of fact, but he was obviously upset. I don't remember what we spoke of as I drove, though I do know I wouldn't have shared my fears with him. Recently I asked Matthew what he remembered of the journey and he said that he was not only desperately worried about his father, but almost equally worried about how I was feeling. It looks as if we travelled in a common pool of misery, trying to comfort each other with feigned optimism. As I struggled to concentrate on following James's directions and not make things worse by getting lost, I couldn't keep questions from coming into my mind. How badly was he hurt? Would he just be undergoing a few routine tests and be home again in a couple of hours? I knew he was conscious, but that didn't mean that there were serious physical injuries. Why, why did he not get out of the car? Fleetingly I regretted that I hadn't given our opera tickets to a neighbour. Oddly enough, years later, I sometimes think of those empty seats and all they symbolise.

We arrived at the hospital sooner than I had expected

and at once saw James and Margaret waving us into a parking space. The next thing I remember is Matthew and me being ushered into a room where Gareth lay on a small, low, stretcher-like bed. He faced away from us, and what I first focused on were his feet, protruding from the bottom of the blanket. One lay flat pointing to the right, and the other equally flat to the left. These unnaturally positioned feet told me in a flash that there was something seriously wrong.

Gareth was very relieved to see Matthew and myself. He was perfectly rational and tried to piece together his jumbled recollections about what happened immediately after the accident. He believed that he must have lost consciousness for a short time, because he remembered a feeling of waking up, grasping the situation and trying to go through safety routines. Although the engine had stalled he wanted to turn off the ignition in case of fire, and his hands wouldn't work. He tried to attract attention by sounding the horn but his fingers couldn't do this either. Eventually he managed to produce the sound by resting the inside of one wrist on the horn and pressing the other hand on top of the first. Next, he wanted to try the brakes and realised at once that he had totally lost the use of his legs. Worst of all, his head was pushed forward onto his chest in an unnatural position, inhibiting breathing, and he was incapable of moving it. He remembered thinking with horror that he must have broken his neck. Then he thought there was a gap before he became conscious that an official of some kind was in the front passenger seat and he managed to whisper, 'Push my head back.'

Now that his head was in a better position, Gareth

remembered his relief that at least he was able to breathe more easily and could gasp directions to the other driver, without realising who he was, to send for an ambulance and get the message through to me. Later again he knew someone was feeling in his pocket for a wallet and realised they were looking for identification. He thought this was a policeman, though Gareth couldn't work out when he arrived. At some other point in time he remembered recognising James and Margaret driving past, a wild hope that they would see him, and relief as they ran towards him.

We didn't learn all this at once, but from time to time Gareth kept returning to what had happened. Obviously his and our main concern was with his present physical condition. He told us that he couldn't move any part of himself except his arms and facial muscles. We were terrified. It was awful beyond description to see Gareth concentrating with all his might to cause a flicker of movement in a finger which remained absolutely still. He persisted in trying to establish his range of sensation by asking us to touch legs, feet and sides. At this stage he was able to say what area we were touching, though the feeling was weak and different from normal. It was obvious that Gareth was desperately worried, as he had been since the first moments after the crash, that he might have broken his neck and would remain paralysed for ever. Matthew and I tried to cheer him up by diverting his thoughts elsewhere, but not surprisingly, with little success. Before long we were asked to withdraw while the medical staff worked on him.

My memories of the time spent at Glangwili are vague and confused. I remember sitting in a little room with

Margaret and James, miserably drinking coffee from a machine and going over and over the situation. They were able to provide encouraging examples of people who had regained movement after paralysis due to an accident. At last they were persuaded to go home when it became evident that there was nothing more they could do. We'd been informed that Gareth could only be kept as comfortable as possible in this hospital and would be transferred to Cardiff Royal Infirmary next morning for specialist treatment. Matthew and I were to be given a room at Glangwili for the night.

Later we were allowed to see Gareth again. He was still wearing a collar for support but also had heavy weights suspended from his head by some kind of pulley system in order to keep his neck in the correct position. This was called traction, we learnt, and was the customary practice for those in Gareth's state. He was in agony from this and there was obviously no means of changing his position to gain some relief. Two sorts of painkillers couldn't dull this severe pain and it was misery to watch. To make matters worse, Gareth's greatest fear was confirmed by an X-ray. We were told that he had indeed broken his neck. Luckily the doctor disclosed this to us both sensitively and gently, so that the full impact didn't hit us then. First, we were told there was every chance that Gareth would make a complete recovery and, secondly, we were totally unable to grasp the full enormity of what it would be like if Gareth were to remain paralysed. Everything was mercifully vague, and in spite of what we had been told, there was a not totally extinguished sense of optimism. When the actual trauma had subsided and the inevitable swelling went down, feeling and movement would return to normal. Perhaps by the morning there would be an improvement . . .

I have absolutely no mental picture of the room in which Matthew and I spent the night. Matthew remembers that I had a bed while he was given blankets for the floor. I don't know if we ate anything that evening or, indeed, the following morning. One thing I do remember is my surprise that I had eventually slept for a few hours. Two worries in particular kept me awake for the greater part of the night. The first concerned the fact that Gareth had a condition called ankylosing spondylitis which had first appeared at the age of nineteen. This was a kind of inflammation of the joints of the spine which gradually caused the vertebrae to become fused. As a result Gareth's neck was at an unusual angle, with his head slightly inclined forward. The question which haunted me was whether the traction was pulling the neck into the wrong position. If this were so, what chance was there that the nerves would find their old pathways? We had of course given the details of the illness to the medical staff, but this wasn't a specialist spinal unit so they may not have encountered the problem before. As it happened, this question was to worry me desperately over the next few days. Even now I have a gnawing suspicion that if Gareth's neck had been fused in exactly his old position the tragedy may, at least partly, have been averted. Obviously this is a 'common sense' – not medically informed – point of view, but such a realisation does nothing to mitigate the torture experienced then and always.

My second worry was about Bethan who had promised to ring us with her friend's telephone number as soon as she arrived in Birmingham. Both she and Matthew had always been meticulous in letting us know where they were, especially when they were out late. It was a rare occurrence that we didn't have this information before she set out and so unfortunate that this emergency should happen now. Bethan knew our intention was to go to the opera and that Matthew might be out for some of the evening, but she also knew that we would be back quite early. She would ring repeatedly until she had allayed my anxiety by letting us know she had arrived safely. At first she would think the opera was longer than expected or that we had been delayed. As time went on she would get more and more worried. There was nothing I could do. The next day I learnt that Bethan had been desperately worried, ringing at intervals until after one o'clock in the morning.

It was a night of misery from which we rose and rushed to find out if Gareth was any better. He was, if anything, in worse pain, due to the traction, which couldn't be removed. The painkillers still hadn't done their job, and the thought of the long journey to Cardiff Royal Infirmary (CRI) was terrifying. The saddest thing, though, was that there was absolutely no return of movement or of sensation. However, he was completely clear-headed and spent much of the short time we were together giving me numerous instructions about the various phone calls I needed to make before following him to Cardiff. Soon the nurses began to prepare Gareth for lifting into the ambulance, and we were asked to leave. Matthew and I hurried out to the Metro and drove home, hoping to get to Cardiff as quickly as possible.

When we reached home I spent the most frustrating

and panic-stricken hour of my entire life. My first task was to contact Bethan. I dashed through our family phone book and failed to find the number. Next I tried to contact a few of her friends whose numbers were in the book in the hope that they could help, but failed again. In despair I began a feverish search of her bedroom. It seemed inevitable that I wouldn't find it – and who could know when we would be at home again? Bethan would be beside herself with worry, yet there was no choice but to get to Cardiff immediately. I worked hopelessly and with shaking hands through the last box-file and astonishingly came upon a scrap of paper on which was written her friend's Christian name and also a phone number. To my infinite relief it was the right one and soon I heard Bethan's voice. I broke the news of the accident and her father's condition in the gentlest way I could, but naturally it was a terrible shock. I remember her saying 'My God, he can't walk?' in horror. I kept repeating the optimistic words of the doctor and advised her to stay in Birmingham and enjoy the rest of the weekend, promising to keep in close touch by phone. In spite of my attempted reassurance she insisted on catching the next train to Cardiff and meeting us at the Infirmary.

With a mixture of relief and unfathomable sorrow I turned to Gareth's instructions. I needed to inform our car insurance firm that the Honda was completely ruined, to tell our solicitor about the accident and to arrange for the AA to collect the remains of the car and take it to our local garage. I wasted anxious minutes finding all the telephone numbers and relevant documents. Luckily, thanks to Gareth, everything was clearly labelled and well-organised. After all this I soon made a discovery which was to become even more significant, namely that late Friday afternoon is the very worst time to have an accident. All these organisations seemed only able to act in office hours, which meant waiting until Monday morning to arrange anything.

I knew this delay would cause Gareth extra, unnecessary worry. In complete frustration Matthew and I grabbed a few essentials and took a hastily summoned taxi to the station. We were just in time to catch an inter-city train which got us to Cardiff in about an hour. It was a sad journey; though we each tried to appear cheerful, neither was deceived. We ran for a taxi and fifteen minutes later entered CRI for the first time. The initial phase of the accident was over and a much harder one was about to begin.

Interlude

Journey to Aberystwyth (1990)

Two not so very young people played on a beach. One stooped, picked up a smooth pebble, tested its weight, then taking up a slip-catching stance tossed it very low to the other. She, adopting a similar stance, dived on to the shingle, just held the catch and quickly returned the pebble at the same height and some way to the right of the man. This continued for some time, each testing the other's reflexes, until they both collapsed laughing and hot. The series of events leading to this tiny incident also led to one of them lying paralysed in hospital some years later.

'I'm thinking of applying for the Chair of Education at Aberystwyth,' was the casual-sounding remark which heralded a different future. There was a stunned silence as the rest of the family digested the implications of this, then uproar.

'Leave our home?'

'Go to a new school?'

'You can't do it, Dad!'

'No, we won't go!'

Patiently Gareth tried to explain why such a move was important to him. He was at the time Reader in Education at Swansea University which meant that there was only one step to the uniquely desirable post of professor – a title carrying in itself implications of substantial academic distinction, not to mention the obvious financial gain. Such a position had always been Gareth's ultimate goal, though in spite of being reasonably confident in his own abilities, he was extremely tentative about his chances of success. His research interests centred on Welsh history so that he was most unlikely to get a chair outside Wales. Now he stressed the rarity of the opportunity, saying that an equivalent one would probably not arise for ages, if at all, in what remained of his professional life. 'I may not get it. I could turn it down if I did. But surely you see I must at least apply!'

What the rest of the family had heard of Aberystwyth was not enticing! We knew all too well of its geographical remoteness worsened by poor road and rail links. How would we be able to keep up present friendships and interests on a regular basis? Also Welsh was the first language for many of the inhabitants. We would feel outsiders when conversing, either simply not understanding or forcing people out of politeness to move from their native tongue. To add to this I could remember one dreary winter's day attending a higher degree ceremony of the University of Wales – as a constituent college of which Aberystwyth was taking its turn to be host. After the moving formalities and the photographing of the splendidly-robed Gareth, we found ourselves looking out on a uniformly bleak scene. As the persistent, drizzling rain soaked our smart clothes, the lifeless sea trickled over harsh pebbles and in the near distance blended with the lowering clouds. This, to me, epitomised Aberystwyth, and my initial reaction to the present proposal was one of dismay.

The real trouble was, however, that our life in Pennard, five minutes ago taken for granted, suddenly seemed perfect. It wasn't only that this was established, familiar, forming life as we knew it, but we really were happy here. Gareth and I had chosen the house twenty-five years before and, since Bethan and Matthew had never lived elsewhere, it held all the memories of their childhood. In every season we had frequented the local Gower beaches and these too held numerous cherished recollections for us. Matthew had settled in the comprehensive school which was about three miles from home and at which Bethan had just embarked on her 'O' level syllabus. Both were involved in many leisure activities which tended to transform Gareth or myself, often both, into chauffeurs of an evening. Their lives were full and solidly based in the security of home – the thought of wiping everything out at once was bewildering.

Gareth tried to be reassuring, filling the alarming vacuum by building up an attractive picture of what would be our future life. Together we would choose a lovely house outside the town with plenty of room for old friends to visit often. There were excellent schools where the children would soon make new friends. Opportunities for music-making would be just as frequent and satisfying. In short, everything would be wonderful! At this time Bethan's burning ambition was to own a horse. Gareth now promised that the chosen house could have enough land to support two horses, one for her and a docile one for me. She was somewhat consoled by the image of her looking through a window and seeing these grazing peacefully. On the other hand, such a thought only deepened Matthew's horror of what he thought his life would be like. In an uncharacteristic and quite-without-hope gesture of defiance, he threatened to camp alone in a tent on the nearby golf links in preference to moving to Aberystwyth.

As for me, I was certain we would move, having long ago experienced two painful pulling up of roots in furtherance of Gareth's career. I was so sure that I didn't apply for a permanent post advertised for the school in which I was on 'teaching practice'. There was no way I could wholly conceal my sorrow at what I thought was a speedily approaching upheaval. I did not want to leave my home – perhaps at some level remembering how the scene of my idyllic childhood was broken up on the early deaths of my parents. I did however say that I was prepared to go since it mattered so much to Gareth.

He applied for the post and the discussion of whether he should accept it if successful dragged on for weeks. Even if not overtly engaged in, it occupied everyone's thoughts most of the time. Then suddenly, with no warning, Gareth made his second startling announcement – he had withdrawn his application! Instead of experiencing a wonderful sense of relief, I was appalled, not least because he had taken this momentous step without telling me first. I begged him to rescind but he said it was too late and anyway that he had made up his mind once and for all. He wouldn't discuss it further and so Gareth was the one who had done the unselfish thing and I was left with the burden of guilt. I kept thinking I should have hidden my real feelings. To make matters worse, the post wasn't filled after interviews with the other short-listed candidates – Gareth would almost certainly have been successful.

Amazingly enough there never were any open

recriminations and four years passed in a fairly uneventful manner. My conscience was increasingly troubled though, as I saw Gareth, for various reasons, growing more and more dissatisfied with his work at Swansea. Then an even more desirable job was advertised for the Aberystwyth Education Department! This time it was for a Research Professor who wouldn't need to run the department but mostly continue with his own writing. It was absolutely perfect for an academic who, like Gareth, was not very enthusiastic about administration but was very enthusiastic indeed about research. Once again he longed to apply and, since a second withdrawal was unthinkable, the initial decision was all-important. It had been hard to live with the thought of a major sacrifice having being made for the sake of the family and I was grateful for the opportunity of cancelling out that earlier negative influence. Bethan, Matthew and I agreed that, however much it went against our own wishes, we must be prepared to move this time. So Gareth applied, was short-listed and finally interviewed in March 1990. Later that day he rang from a Wrexham hotel where he was spending a night after a school visit. He had unofficially just been told the outcome of the interview. I knew at once from the exhilaration so markedly present in his voice that he'd been successful. Luckily I quite surprised myself with the glad spontaneity of my reaction to his complete happiness.

When we turned to practical details the next day, we decided to keep our Pennard home until Matthew had completed his 'A' levels at Gorseinon College and chosen a university. Bethan was already at Bristol University so was away from home much of the time. Gareth now needed to find a temporary home in Aberystwyth for most week-nights. It wasn't an ideal situation for any of us, but it would do. Optimistically, he thought he would work late in college during the week and be able to spend time relaxing with the family at weekends.

It wasn't very easy to find a suitable place, however. At first Gareth thought to take lodgings but quite soon realised he wouldn't be able to face having a landlady at his age. Even thirty years earlier as a young student he'd resented some of the inevitable restrictions of living in 'digs' and I can well remember his blind fury when on one occasion he'd been reprimanded for being late for a meal. Flats for hire seemed to be few in number and those that were tolerable were expensive. Rather than waste money on rent we decided to buy something small, hoping it would be a useful investment which could be exchanged for a family home in a year or two. At length Gareth found a second-floor, two-bedroomed, new flat alongside the river Rheidol just before it flows into the sea. It was part of a complex originally designed as retirement homes. The communal areas, including the lift, grounds and car park, were serviced on payment of an annual fee, so we would only have the actual flat to look after. It would never get really cold when left empty in the winter, sandwiched as it was between other flats. Best of all, it was only a five-minute walk to work, across the bridge which spanned the river and through the old streets to the sea front and Old College. Gareth would not risk all our savings on the deposit on this flat until I had seen and approved it, so he arranged for us both to meet the estate agent involved at the earliest possible date.

The day had started with Gareth and myself, each thinking the other slept, lying side by side pondering over the epoch-making decisions which lay ahead. 'Please let Kath fall for Aber!' was Gareth's recurrent wish. Considering the emotionally-loaded nature of the whole debate about moving, I found myself in a surprisingly calm and positive frame of mind. 'I will like Aber, or if I don't, will pretend to like it!' was my persistent refrain. An objective observer privy to our thoughts would have felt optimistic about the outcome.

No wonder we were happy as we drove along. The weather could not have been better and the rural scenery was astonishingly lovely. Once we got on to smaller roads, fields stretched for miles and miles on either side and we could see distant hills in sharp detail. Further on, these roads became tortuous and undulating, so we cornered, climbed and descended sharply, all in quick succession. The surrounding countryside became more dramatic, perhaps even more breathtakingly beautiful. We were neither trapped behind a slow and bulky tractor nor did we come across an impassable flock of sheep – both common hazards on this route. But even if we had, it wouldn't have mattered: we shared an uncanny belief that this was our day and nothing could mar it. Gareth insisted we stopped about half way at a roadside cafe called *Pig'n Piglets*. A talkative mynah bird greeted us and threw seed far and wide as we drank our coffee. Today this seemed charming.

There isn't one reasonably fast and straightforward route from Swansea to Aberystwyth. Instead there are numerous, rather complicated, cross-country options and everybody seems to have a favourite, comparisons of which are a very popular topic of conversation. For my first experience of this journey Gareth had chosen the slightly longer coastal road. He drove quite slowly so we could receive the full impact of the stunning views of the shore-line and beyond into Cardigan Bay. We went through the little holiday town of Aberaeron, well supplied with caravan parks, and I remembered an old friend was wont to enthuse about happy weeks spent here long ago. This reminded Gareth of childhood holidays with his parents in Aberystwyth and time passed both happily and quickly so that I was surprised to find we had arrived at the flat.

The estate agent was waiting in the car park and she took us up in the lift to another flat on the second floor. It had a balcony overlooking the river and, consequently, was ten thousand pounds more expensive than ours. We sipped sherry and nibbled peanuts before being led across the corridor to the smaller flat. Gareth's descriptive powers had left me with no visual image of what it would be like and it far exceeded my expectations. It is true it looked bare compared with the one we had just left: the second bedroom was tiny and all we could see from the windows was a shale wall. (The builders had apparently promised to spray this with some sort of artificial greenery and, although this was never done, it became covered with many kinds of wild plants in a remarkably short space of time.) Nevertheless the whole place was bright and functional. The kitchen and bathroom were beautifully designed and equipped to a standard higher than their equivalent in Pennard. It would be quite big enough for the four of us to be very comfortable for short periods and perfect for Gareth during the week.

Feeling reckless we signed the contract and spent half an hour measuring for curtains. It was still hard to accept that this actually was another home for us, one that should make all our hopes for the immediate future a reality. Gareth was always desperately worried about keeping the family solvent and went a few times through the argument about the flat being an investment before being able to push it out of his mind so that we could begin to explore the immediate vicinity. After wandering down to the river and across the bridge to the harbour, Gareth took me on what would be his daily walk to Old College. The streets were narrow and congested and we were glad to reach the beach. Having thrown pebbles to each other for a while, we walked to the water's edge and played 'ducks and drakes'. Both of us returned to childhood whenever we were at the seaside, but today we were particularly light-headed with happiness. Tired out at last we lay on the shingle in the strong sunshine until tempted by the tune of an ice-cream van. As we ate our 'ninety nines' we investigated the ruins of the castle which overlooked the sea. Then we walked along the promenade in the opposite direction until we 'kicked the bar' – a time-honoured tradition of Aberystwyth students. We were seeing the town in all its summer glory and felt nowhere could be lovelier. How, I wondered, could I have built up such a misguided image of the place? Who had told me such fables? Old College, intriguing and imposing, towered above the beach, a solid symbol of Gareth's professional satisfaction.

As we drove contentedly back to Pennard we envisaged a dazzlingly happy future. Not only would Gareth have a convenient and comfortable base but the whole family would enjoy it for the occasional weekend and holiday. He hadn't thought to mention that the flat was right next to a river, though I was enchanted by this and could hardly believe he saw it as a minor feature! We would buy a small dinghy and row down the river to the harbour when Bethan and Matthew were with us. Also we would explore the inland countryside and the famous coastline. No longer would we drive everywhere but take long, health-giving walks. Everything was new, exciting and above all enticing. We saw so clearly a stimulating, positive way of life in this environment which need not involve breaking strong links with the past.

The central feature was Gareth's delight at his promotion – he knew he would revel in the challenges that faced him. Above all he was almost overcome by the immense relief at having balanced the conflicting interests of home and career. Obviously there were further decisions to be made at the end of the year, but we were wholly confident all would be well. Almost for the first time we saw that it would be possible for the two of us, when the children had their own homes and lives, to become integrated into a different, friendly society – with only ourselves to consider. The overwhelmingly negative image of such a time began to brighten a little.

There were many other journeys to Aberystwyth; for instance, the next one, when we loaded the Honda to its roof and partially furnished the flat. Carpets had been laid and beds delivered. I had bought curtains and bedding in Swansea and we ransacked the house for crockery, cutlery, cooking utensils and cleaning equipment. We took two smallish armchairs, coffee tables, a black and white ancient television and numerous other things. By the end of this visit our second home was habitable, if rather bare. Again we drove home well-pleased with our efforts, but never would we be able to regain the glowing splendour of that first journey. Then we knew with absolute confidence that we were impregnable, a family immune to misfortune – how ironic that, inadvertently, we had made terrible tragedy possible.

2

Thomas Andrew Ward

The taxi drew up outside the tiny, crowded car park of Cardiff Royal Infirmary. Matthew and I jumped out in a panic and dashed through the unimpressive entrance. A porter leaned on the counter just inside and I asked him breathlessly where we would find an accident victim brought from west Wales that morning. He immediately referred to lists on his computer and at first drew a blank. My spirits sank yet further as it seemed doubtful whether we would ever identify Gareth's whereabouts in what appeared to be a huge, amorphous building. However, after a minute or two we were directed along a crowded corridor, up in a lift and along another corridor to Thomas Andrew Ward. We hovered uncertainly outside for half a minute then advanced stoically, bracing ourselves against the unspeakable horrors probably waiting within.

A young male nurse was busy in the office/observation post just inside the door. He greeted us pleasantly and pointed to the nearest bed. There lay Gareth, very, very, pleased to see us, but in a sorry state. He looked even less like his usual self than at Glangwili. Now, weights adding up to fourteen pounds as traction were fitted by a scissors-like contraption to his skull. The relevant areas had been shaved and there was blood on the scalp. He had a firm, large collar supporting the neck and an oxygen mask fitted to cover mouth and nose. Finally there were 'lines' attached to various parts of his body by sticky pads or by needles under the skin held in place by plasters. Matthew and I took in these details with a horror which we tried to conceal as we expressed our relief at finding him.

Gareth, as throughout, was perfectly rational. He told us how he had reached the hospital only an hour ago, how he had been wheeled into the ward, transferred into a bed and made 'comfortable' – he was even able to manage a sort of wry grin at the debased meaning of this word! In fact he was in severe pain which grew worse no matter how many painkillers he was allowed. He described the journey which had been excruciating in spite of the ambulance driver's slow speed and care. It was a route Gareth knew well and, though flat on his back and unable to move his head, he recognised every roundabout. The time had seemed endless. Next, as urgently as the oxygen mask would allow, he asked for the results of my list of phone calls. His only comfort was that I had managed to contact Bethan and he was very touched that she had insisted on leaving her friends. But just as I had anticipated, he was very discouraged at the lack of information from all the institutions I had tried to contact. Sadly he accepted that we would simply have to wait until Monday. As we three chatted, trying to come to terms with the appalling situation in which we found ourselves, we suddenly saw Bethan enter the ward. As much as was visible of Gareth's face brightened momentarily. It was wonderful to see her – the whole family would confront the disaster together.

It was a dreadful shock for Bethan to see her father

with all the paraphernalia of serious injury – having to take the full impact in one instant. Matthew and I hastily repeated all the encouraging information we had been given and Bethan adjusted to the pseudo-optimistic atmosphere in no time at all. The four of us went over the full story of the accident and the explanation of our failure to contact her the previous evening. Bethan made light of her panic throughout the night and tried to take our attention away from the immediate situation with news of the friends she had been with at Birmingham, most of whom we had met.

It was no good, though. Despite every effort to divert each other we were all obsessed with the question of whether the paralysis would remain. Gareth was still unable to move any part of his body below chest level. The collar, obviously, stopped any neck movement. This meant he could only control his face, his arms and, to a very small extent, his hands. It was piteous to see him willing his limbs to move but nothing happening. (Many years earlier in philosophy classes I had puzzled over the problem of how the 'mental' activity of willing could result in a physical action – how terrible to see this connection broken down. How impossible to grasp that willing to move a foot could produce nothing. The temptation was to say 'Try harder, it must work' – nobody did.) Even worse was carrying out Gareth's instructions to touch different parts of his body to check that at least some sensation remained in areas he was unable to move. Matthew and I had done this repeatedly at Glangwili and hoped for some improvement. We were asked, for instance, to touch one foot and Gareth would then say which it was. Sometimes he got it wrong and we didn't know whether to tell him – it seemed so cruel to confirm his, and our, worst fears. After all he did often get it right, yet it isn't the sort of thing that should ever be got wrong under 'normal' conditions. A terrible suspicion began to grow in the minds of Matthew and myself, that Gareth's remaining sensations were getting weaker.

The nursing staff of Thomas Andrew were very tolerant, letting all of us stay in the ward throughout the day. Sometimes we were asked to move to a small patients' day-room whilst they attended to Gareth. This contained a temperamental television, some chairs and a pervasive smell of smoke. However, we were never kept away from the ward for long – a fact for which we were most grateful. The man we had judged earlier to be in charge was particularly friendly. He, in line with hospital policy, asked us to call him by his forename, Salim. Nearly every time we passed him one of us had a question relating to Gareth's condition. Seeing how frightened we were he explained that ninety-five per cent of patients who were admitted paralysed regained at least some feeling and movement within a few days, often within twenty-four hours. Almost always, he said, there was complete recovery over time. You can imagine how our optimism grew, how enthusiastically as a family we repeated his words, sensing an end to the nightmare of the last night and day. Yet time seemed to stand still as we watched Gareth's pain increase. The traction became absolute agony and the staff could only decrease the weights a little. The hard collar cut remorselessly into his skin at several places and this couldn't be alleviated. Another new sort of pain-killer was simply not strong enough to cope.

All this time since he had been settled on the ward, Gareth had been seen by no one more senior than Salim who was probably a staff nurse. Quite early on I asked him when a specialist would conduct an examination. Here my earlier suspicion was confirmed, that late Friday was the worst possible time to be injured or taken ill. The consultants were simply not available over the weekend. (This may not have been true in every case or of every department in the hospital.) Certainly Gareth wouldn't be seen until some time on Monday. We were utterly dismayed, seeing the state that he was in and realising he would continue to suffer like this for one whole day and two nights. Besides, we wanted something to be done to combat the paralysis – not just a continuation of the waiting game begun at Glangwili. Even at this stage we feared that these lost days could be crucial to the return of movement.

As the dreary day crawled towards evening, Matthew, Bethan and I simply assumed we would stay with Gareth. It seems odd and amazingly stupid of me to have had no thought of any alternative course of action or, indeed, to wonder where we might sleep. There was certainly no thought that any of us might go home to Swansea. I did at least ring a neighbour to ask her to feed our cat until further notice. Out of the blue a nurse came to tell us that the hospital had a few rooms designed to accommodate the families of patients who were seriously ill. These were allocated to those who lived comparatively far away and we were being offered one. We were touched and infinitely grateful, then shortly after were taken to a small, narrow room with one single bed, and given extra bedding for those who would sleep on the floor. This answered our needs wonderfully – it would have been awful to see funds wasted on providing luxurious sleeping places – but such basic provision redounds to the credit of the hospital.

I refused to leave Gareth that night. Matthew had already spent one night in misery at Glangwili so I insisted he got some sleep and eventually he settled on the floor of our room. Bethan too was looking exhausted after her short, worried night but decided she would set the alarm on her watch and come to check how her father was at four o'clock in the morning. I could not dissuade her, and we promised Matthew we would come for him if necessary. Secretly I hoped they would both sleep through. The night staff were rather surprised at my decision, but made no attempt to change my mind. At the time I wasn't particularly grateful, but now, with a far greater knowledge of hospitals, I realise how lucky I was. Nothing would have moved me from that ward, but I was spared fighting for the right to stay with my husband. One of the nurses brought me an armchair from somewhere; another example of the kindness beyond the call of duty we experienced in Thomas Andrew. The patients were all prepared for the night, the lights were dimmed and silence settled on the ward, only interrupted by the occasional quiet movement of nurses. It was a terrible night – hour after hour of watching Gareth in severe pain and everyone being totally unable to do anything about it. Sometimes he fell into a fitful sleep but was conscious most of the time. The nurses came to change his position slightly every so often and provided as many painkillers as they dared. The torment of the paralysis question was ever present, but for the most part, was overwhelmed by the sheer horror of the physical pain. At about three o'clock Bethan, pale but determined, appeared at the bedside. Gareth had just sunk into a deeper sleep, the drugs taking effect at last. I was persuaded to return to our little room to sleep for a few hours on condition that Bethan would wake me if the pain got worse again.

Exhausted by misery I did sleep immediately and was woken by the alarm at seven. Matthew and I hurried along the increasingly familiar corridors to Thomas Andrew where Bethan talked to her father. He, true to character, was worrying over immediate practical problems such as the car, insurance and medical cover. Behind these lay the deeper worries. If he remained paralysed, how could he work? How would we live? Would we have to sell the house? How could we support both children at university? Such questions expressed the possibility of the end of the secure life we had so carefully built up over nearly thirty years. He tried not to discuss these implications of permanent paralysis too often, especially when Bethan and Matthew were around, but there is no doubt that these forebodings never left his mind, adding to the physical torment.

However there was no way of avoiding the central question on which all these doubts about the future turned. Would the paralysis remain? From early morning Gareth resumed the practice of frequently asking all three of us in turn to touch his feet, legs and sides. It became horribly obvious that he had now lost all sensation below chest level. We touched, poked and even pinched in our desperation to get a response, but there never was the slightest recognition of the stimulus. This deterioration since yesterday seemed a clear sign-post to tragedy. I began to think that the treatment which had only involved applying traction must have been somehow wrong if Gareth was getting worse. I spoke to Salim who was again in charge of the ward, and he assured me that traction was always used and he did not think it could be doing any harm. Yet the fact of Gareth's unusual neck angle due to his spondylitis continued to prey on my mind. For the thousandth time I asked myself how, if the neck were stretched to a new position, the old nerve pathways could re-establish themselves? Clearly we needed expert advice but knew there was no hope of seeing a consultant for twenty-four hours. The frustration at seeing time being wasted which could possibly save Gareth from being crippled for ever became intolerable. (I have heard since that new research in America has shown that the period immediately after the accident is of vital importance for recovery, and experimental procedures at the actual scene of the disaster are being introduced. So what hope is there two and a half days later?) As time went on and the general depression of the whole family deepened, I determined to overcome my natural reluctance to interfere in this unfamiliar and frightening environment. Somehow or another an expert must be found. I searched for Salim and explained my fears once again. He said kindly that he would summon a superior but that it would not be a consultant.

A little later I was ushered into the small office at the entry to the ward for my one and only encounter with the duty registrar. Nothing short of desperation had got me there and I hardly dared lift my eyes to this person who might save Gareth. He was youngish, dark-haired and of medium height, but the only thing that seemed of significance, and immediately deepened my despair yet further, was the fact that clearly I was not face to face with a concerned, friendly professional. He lounged at his ease against the corner of a filing cabinet, stared at me coldly and greeted me with, 'Tell me the situation as you see it.' He did not shake hands, introduce himself or ask me to sit down. Throughout the interview I stood forlornly just inside the door.

Perhaps sympathy would have reduced me to tears; in the event I was forced to brace myself against this unnerving antagonism. Certainly at the time I was beyond wondering why he behaved so rudely. Somehow I managed to give what I hope was a lucid account of the injury, treatment and, in particular, my fear that Gareth's unusual pre-accident condition necessitated special attention. I stressed that his obvious deterioration in twenty-four hours had made me desperately worried that his treatment may, by holding his neck in the wrong position, be making him worse. The registrar listened, seemingly in an idle and inattentive manner, and at the end of the pitiful narrative glanced casually in my direction and with no hint of sympathy in his voice said bluntly, 'I have to tell you that your husband will never walk again.'

How can I describe the impact of this blow so callously given? The very worst of the fears we had all been rehearsing ever since the accident had been completely verified. Our lives were irretrievably ruined and I was left with a blurred, black sense of the future. Struggling desperately for some clearer grasp of the implications of his bald statement, I lost sight of my original query about alternative treatment and uttered a few of the thoughts of despair which quickly succeeded each other in my stunned mind, 'Will Gareth die? What sort of life will he live if he survives? What can I do? What can any of us do?' The registrar looked bored, rustled some papers and was obviously eager to leave. He made no attempt to help me understand or even come to terms with Gareth's condition. Soon he brushed past me and opened the door, implying the interview was over.

Just at that moment I was overwhelmed by the thought of what the killing of all hope would do to Gareth, and also Bethan and Matthew. They must not be tortured by the words of this brute, now or ever. At least such profound cruelty continued to stop me breaking down and, gathering up the shattered remains of my determination, I ignored the open door and faced the fact that I must beg a favour even of such a man: 'I ask you to do one thing for me. Don't tell my husband or my children what you have just told me.' Totally unconcerned he postured and pretended to hesitate: 'Alright, but I don't like it.' He still stood by the door, holding it open, and with an unmistakable gesture finally got me outside. He left, having spent no more than a few minutes with me. As I stood, fighting for self-control, I caught a glimpse of Salim's face, utterly aghast at what he had witnessed. I don't think it was because he himself had predicted the opposite, more optimistic, outcome; rather that he, unlike the registrar, was able to understand and sympathise with our intense suffering. Yet in such a hierarchical institution he could never say to his superior 'You've got it wrong. She's not a trouble maker, but is simply and desperately seeking help.'

Once the duty registrar had made his view plain, I was

trying to accept the fact of Gareth's permanent paralysis and cope with it, rather than questioning the grounds on which his judgement was based or fighting his complete indifference. I emerged from that office with my terrible secret and with hardly a dozen paces to the bed where he lay being 'kept cheerful' by Bethan and Matthew. As far as I was concerned all hope was gone, but I was absolutely sure that it was too soon for Gareth to face the certainty of never walking again. It seemed kinder to let hope dwindle gradually, at least for the near future. This may not have been the 'right' decision – I was acting purely instinctively – but I stand by what I did to this day. The others had been waiting anxiously for me to return, hoping for good news or at least useful advice. Eager voices demanded, 'What did he say? Can something be done? Will he help Dad get better?' Knowing I had to quench that optimism was bad enough: having to conceal the truth was worse. As neutrally as I could I said that the registrar had been unsympathetic and uninformative, so we would have to wait for the next day. They accepted this sadly and time again dragged on interminably. Nobody noticed there was a change in the quality of my despair – after all at best we three put on what were obviously assumed brave faces. However, whenever anyone made a hopeful remark, my sickening knowledge was almost too much to bear.

This new turn of events deepened my worry about the effect all their recent experiences were having on Bethan and Matthew. They had already spent long hours at their father's bedside, not only coming to terms with the state he was in, but also seeing everything else that happened in a full and varied ward. Gareth was not the only patient to be in a poor condition. In spite of the efforts of the staff it was a depressing place. I now knew they would suffer even more intensely when, at some point in time, they learnt there would be no recovery from the paralysis.

However desperately he worried about his own situation, Gareth could never lessen his concern for our children. Throughout the terrible day he and I found moments to discuss what could be done for them to keep some modicum of 'normal' life. We knew all too well that both were particularly at risk of damage from the situation. Matthew was always very sensitive to human and animal suffering. He has been a strict vegetarian since the age of ten and is strongly against the use of animals in the testing of household products, cosmetics, food and even drugs. For some years he 'busked' on his violin in the streets of Swansea when he had time and always sent all the gifts of the generous shoppers to charities (£500 one Christmas Eve). He tended to get very involved with children he knew to be unhappy. (For example, when he was in junior school, I remember my predicament when he came to me in all confidence for food and blankets for a child who intended to run away from home.) As he grew older he befriended and tried to help one or two youngsters with serious difficulties. Bethan, in her creative writing and response to literature, as in life, had from her earliest years shown exceptional sensitivity to the feelings of others. It had always been impossible, to the extent we wished, to protect her from the tension or unhappiness experienced by those around her. She somehow sensed something was wrong and struggled with all her youthful might to make things right again. If Gareth and I were ever at odds, it was, as likely as not, concern for Bethan that would make us sort things out!

Our first attempt at providing the youngsters with a break took the form of managing to persuade Bethan to attend a special session of her karate club which was to end with a barbecue that evening. She absolutely refused to leave the hospital for any length of time, but Swansea was only fifty miles away so she could get back before midnight. We knew she had been looking forward to this so were very pleased when she managed to arrange for a close friend to pick her up at the station and take her home to collect her *gi* before training started. It all went according to plan. Apparently everyone was warmly concerned, offering help in any possible way. However she couldn't bear to stay for the barbecue, her mind being full of images of her father, and rushed back to hospital. It was at least a partial success; she did have a short break. We would build on this.

We had much more persuading to do in Matthew's case. He had been chosen to attend a week's course at Villiers Park, Oxford. Students were selected from all over the country for intensive study of a particular subject, music in Matthew's case. This was quite an honour and was intended to give sixth formers at the end of their first year of 'A' levels a taste of university life. Gareth was absolutely determined that Matthew should not miss this unique opportunity. It was very difficult indeed to make Matthew see that the best thing he could do for his father was to go. We argued that at least Gareth would then have something optimistic to think about that might cheer him up when all else failed. Matthew would not be far away and we could phone as often as he liked.

If we needed him he could be back in not much more than an hour. At last Matthew agreed, but the next question was how on earth could we get him ready? The only solution was for Matthew and me to dash home at some point the next day, if the long-expected expert judged it safe for me to leave for a few hours.

In the meantime, though my secret knowledge that Gareth would never get better weighed intolerably on my mind, though we were all fixated on the central terror of paralysis, though we were tormented with worry about the future, we were getting acclimatised to living around Gareth's bed. Sunday had been a depressing, worrying day, not just because of the behaviour and message of the registrar, but because of learning more about – and even sometimes recognising changes in – Gareth's condition. For instance we rejoiced with Gareth at the removal of the hated traction earlier in the day, only to see it replaced with what was alleged to be a stronger but more comfortable collar. In a very short time it rubbed his neck and face raw in several places. It seemed as if the choice was between traction and a very stiff collar, each causing awful pain which mingled with the constant ache around the area of the break. Another cause for concern was that gradually Gareth's ability to breathe was changing. He had become more or less resigned to the wearing of an oxygen mask, though he still tended to panic at its restriction, especially since his inability to move meant he couldn't tear it off if he felt desperate. Towards evening he could hardly draw breath. He tried to alleviate this by inhaling more deeply from the mask tied tightly by elastic at the back of his head but with little success. Would this get worse, and if so, where would the deterioration end?

Gareth had always been quite strong physically, especially in his arms. As he lay completely inert, for the first time ever he seemed too fragile to touch – disturbing to a wife and children. We saw the nurses handling him with the care suited to a new-born baby. Gradually through this second day in hospital, we began to understand the reason for this delicacy and with it to learn about the wearisome business of skin care for paralysed people. One of the nurses, called Janet, explained that they did not slightly change Gareth's position every couple of hours just for his comfort, far from it. Since he was completely unable to move his body, it would take an alarmingly short time for the skin on the 'pressure areas' to become inflamed and a sore develop. Gareth wouldn't feel any of this, hence the danger. Sometimes plastic surgery is needed for these sores and, usually, months of avoiding putting pressure on the affected area, so the patient tends to be bed-ridden until it clears. In extreme cases it can even result in death. I was terrified by this and wondered why Janet, usually so sensitive, was going into so much depressing detail at this stage. No doubt she too believed Gareth to be permanently paralysed. She explained that avoidance of sores was the main aspect of patient care that families had to learn and put into practice – 'never too soon to start!' she said cheerily. 'You'll have to keep a close eye on all pressure areas day and night.' As a favour I was invited to stay behind the curtains drawn to screen his bed when Gareth was 'turned' next. Feeling cowardly at the time I saw this as a doubtful privilege, but took up my station at the foot of the bed. Jane called three other busy nurses from far and wide. They lined up with their hands positioned evenly underneath and along the whole length of Gareth's body. Jane counted to three and together they gently turned him marginally away from them taking the greatest care that the angle of his head relative to his neck did not change. The sheets were tweaked to a condition of absolute smoothness to avoid creases damaging the skin, and pillows placed between the legs and down both sides of his body to hold him absolutely still. Janet pulled open the curtains around the bed and smiled brightly at me, perhaps expecting to be thanked, but got only a pale acknowledgement. I had seen too devastating a glimpse of what the future might hold and a vivid imagination filled in other details.

Another crushing consequence of the accident was incontinence. The nurse had explained this was all part of the loss of muscle control below chest level and that Gareth would need to be catheterised. At the time this meant virtually nothing, but again by this second day we had partly got used to a tube leading from the bladder and the employment of urine-drainage bags. As virtually permanent features of the ward, members of the family were allowed to empty these into special, calibrated bottles when a certain volume was reached. I was glad to be useful but the necessity for it was profoundly disquieting. Also since there was a permanent fear of dehydration, we were asked to help by giving Gareth as much water as he would drink. We used 'bendy' straws and persuaded him to sip a little, poking the straw through the oxygen mask. Obviously he was unable to feed himself and again we could be useful in spooning small amounts of hospital food into that reluctant mouth.

So this was my husband who, two days earlier, had

been running a university department. I now saw him lying absolutely helpless, his neck encased in a big collar, many 'lines' connected to different skin areas, oxygen being pumped into his lungs, a catheter emerging from his body, a device attached to his finger to monitor the amount of oxygen that was being absorbed into his blood and, worst of all, he was in constant pain. I had been told he would not get better. A frightening picture of what our lives would be like was beginning to emerge. In spite of grim forebodings the other three still had some hope. I faced a future with a permanently paralysed husband and found it hard to join in the forced, optimistic banter with which Bethan and Matthew tried to cheer us all up.

Interlude

Italy – Motor-Rail (1995)

Two cars, between them holding six people, squeezed through a narrow iron gate and parked in front of a villa. The Italian owner and his wife instantly appeared, smiling a warm welcome. This was near Montaione, a village in Tuscany. It was still pleasantly hot, though it was quite late in the afternoon and some of the party longed to try out the large pool. The older, more solemn element were anxiously asking the way to the nearest supermarket before closing time. All this was so typical of the beginning of a magical two weeks in the sun.

Being confined to a wheelchair has made an incalculable difference to every aspect of Gareth's life. Nothing illustrates this more clearly than our attempts to carry on the long-established practice of taking one foreign holiday a year. Perhaps such an aim would seem to be of minor significance, yet it is an essential part of trying to establish some continuity between before and after the accident. We have at least to pretend to be the same people doing the same things. What used to be a comparatively simple matter of choice and finance is now a complex, often demoralising and sometimes even dangerous struggle.

In the summer of the year previous to our Italian holiday I had found driving to the south of France exhausting, so now we had decided to try the French-run Motor Rail, relishing the image of the family sleeping cosily in couchettes whilst the same train also carried the car the full length of France. After spending a night at Dover we took the ferry to Calais, the Motor Rail terminus. Disabled passengers travelling by cross-channel ferry are usually treated with great care, instructions being relayed to the loading crew from the check-in point. I was waved aboard eventually and stopped at the bottom of a narrow and steep ramp, seeing the car in front was parked towards the top of it and its occupants collecting their possessions together. One of the loaders indicated that I was to follow suit. To his annoyance, I refused, explaining that, since the wheelchair could only be got out of the side of the car, Gareth would be stuck inside. Any cars coming in behind us would then have to be unloaded again for us to reverse, since no-one is allowed to stay on the car-deck during the voyage. He was a Frenchman with little English, and it took a demonstration of the chair-lifting mechanism for him to understand the problem and his Gallic charm to be restored. Anyway we reached Calais and I looked forward to a day free from driving.

Soon we met up with one of my sisters and her husband with a great increase of holiday spirits. They had come with us the previous year to give us confidence on our first foreign holiday since Gareth's accident. At that time Bethan and Matthew could only fly out to join us for the second week, due to musical commitments. This year we were lucky to have them both for the whole time. Now the six of us decided to have a celebratory snack since we were early and, luckily, the only cafe in the depot was wheelchair accessible, though there were a few hazards to overcome. After much discussion we chose one fairly basic cake each, together with fizzy drinks or coffee. To our surprise it cost well over twenty pounds. We bore it bravely – after all we were on holiday – but made plans to stock up in an Italian supermarket for the return journey.

There was still nearly an hour to go but we thought it as well to find out the procedures for getting a wheelchair-bound passenger on to the train. Both Gareth and I had rung Motor Rail on various occasions, asking for the width of the doorways and the height of the steps leading up to the train. We never had any precise answers to our questions but were assured each time that wheelchair passengers were conveyed safely and without problems every day. It took us a while to find an official, but eventually we were told that Gareth must use one of their wheelchairs to be taken down to the train. This seemed an unnecessary though not unreasonable request, so we asked for a chair straight away. We needed to carry out the undignified and quite difficult task of lifting Gareth from one wheelchair to another, outside, in the middle of a group of strangers. However, the key to the hut which housed their wheelchairs couldn't be found, so after about half an hour of searching, a pleasant lady escorted Gareth in his own electric chair down to the loading platform. This was a considerable distance and involved bumping over railway tracks with wooden insets. Foot passengers, having disposed of their cars, walked another way. I had to leave Gareth and run back to find out what to do with the car. In fact this only involved handing in a labelled key after which it would be driven on to the train for us.

Before long our group stood together at the side of the train and turned our attention to the question of getting Gareth aboard. I looked up and up to the doorway of a typical French train. There was no ramp, no way of lifting the chair, and the doorway was far too narrow. An advance party identified our cabin and saw with dismay that it was quite a way from the door, down a corridor that was also narrow. In great concern we called back our escort. She looked at Gareth and said, 'Can't he stand to get on?' In unison several of our party gave emphatic and annoyed 'Nos,' while I added, 'That's why he's in a wheelchair.' The only solution was to lift him from the chair like a sack of potatoes and bundle him through the narrow doorway and corridor to the cabin. There was only room for one person to lift him under the shoulders while someone else bore the weight of the legs. It was a terrible strain to lift an adult up steps and some distance along the corridor in this way. There was no-one from Motor Rail to help and it was as well my brother-in-law and our children were strong. Many families wouldn't have been able to cope.

The cabins were of the old-fashioned British Rail corridor type with two facing, continuous, parallel benches. Since his accident, for the protection of his skin, Gareth needed to sit on a Ro-ho cushion, which was made of soft plastic and was filled with air. This was always kept in his wheelchair. I had brought with us in case of emergency a sort of padded cushion with sides, lent by our kind senior district nurse. We put this in a corner of the carriage and gently lowered Gareth on to it. He has no sense of balance now and, though his feet rested naturally on the floor, he kept slumping sideways or forward. I sat close to him for support, propping him upright, but it wasn't exactly comfortable for either of us! This, then, was the start of a fifteen-hour journey. Gareth was not only extremely uncomfortable, but very downcast – filled with grim forebodings about the chances of his surviving the journey in a reasonably healthy state.

The chair, we were told, would be lifted on further down the train and re-united with Gareth when we reached Bologna. This was a constant worry. On the present record how could we believe (a) it was on the train, (b) that it was intact since, for instance, Ro-ho and footplates were detachable, (c) that if it were aboard it wouldn't be unloaded at random anywhere through the night, and (d) that it would appear at Bologna? Bethan and Matthew walked a long way down the corridor, eventually coming upon the chair abandoned just inside a door, unlabelled and unprotected. Without this chair we would be in the deepest trouble, and in our wildest moments, we visualised Gareth being flown home to spend months in hospital with bed-sores.

After a while we all calmed down, shared out what we had to eat and drink, and decided we had to forget the chair and assume all would be well. We chatted and played word-games, a little of the holiday spirit reviving from its all-but-certain death. Time wore on and someone raised the hitherto suppressed question of how we were to sleep. We could all six of us sit, three a side, but how lie? Again all our repeated requests for information had been unproductive and, mistakenly as it turned out, we had assumed there would be three couchettes, each to cater for two people. When our documents were being checked, the official showed us how the backs of the bench seats were raised to form a second tier of bunks and a third set was constructed above. All six of us were to sleep in this tiny space! At least no strangers were involved, but they could have been. Perhaps in pre-accident days we would have laughed and enjoyed the proximity of the rest of the family, but now I had a paralysed person to deal with. At intervals throughout the day we had cleared one of the benches for Gareth to lie down for an hour to keep pressure sores at bay, but Bethan had helped me lift then and the middle bunk was not in position to impede us.

Before ten o'clock we assembled the bunks and stuffed the duvets and pillows into the fresh cases provided. The able-bodied of our party took it in turns to use the fairly basic washing facilities while I dampened a flannel for Gareth and used a drop of bottled water for him to clean his teeth. There was no question of my removing his clothes and we hoped this wouldn't cause skin problems. I had brought a sleeping bag and we spread this on one of the lower bunks on top of the foam cushion which we spread out to cover as big an area as possible. Bethan and I hauled Gareth on to this, somehow turning him to face outwards. We couldn't be sure he was secure and the sleeping bag was rather slippery. One of my main worries since he had been man-handled onto the train was that the continence apparatus had been disturbed. From time to time I had checked this surreptitiously, being keenly aware of Gareth's loss of dignity, and emptied the leg bag when no one seemed to be looking. Now a night-bag had to be attached and suspended so that the liquid would flow unimpeded. Any resistance and we were in for floods, wet clothes and a major clean-up operation. No acid could be allowed to stay in contact with Gareth's skin. I had packed a relatively small bag of equipment to get over this fairly frequent disaster but had counted on a private couchette. Nobody but the immediate family knew the precise nature of these problems and we wanted to keep it this way. Gareth and I were acutely aware of how difficult it would be, with four other people extremely close, inadequate lighting, water some way away and impossible handling conditions. Anyway, Bethan and Matthew climbed up to the top bunks, my sister and her husband took the middle ones and we settled for a few hours.

It was very hot and we were scarcely surprised to find that the air-conditioning was not working. There was a small, high window but this didn't seem to make any difference. In any case I could hardly sleep with Gareth a few feet away likely to fall on the floor, and got very tense, fearing I wouldn't be in a fit state to drive safely the next morning. I had decided to change his position more often than usual because of the dubious surface on which he was sleeping. At about two o'clock, using the slippery sleeping bag I was able to turn Gareth to face inwards. Since there was no gap between the bench and the wall, it was impossible to check that the continence arrangements were still secure. I had in the end just to hope for the best. We tried to sleep again and may have dozed a little, but at half-past four it was time to turn him over again. With no access to the inner side of the bunk, how could I turn him towards me without his falling off? I reached over and pushed, pulled and struggled, trying not to wake the others, until at last he was in place. It was then I found that the worst had happened and that everything would probably be soaked in urine. In panic I rummaged in my bag to find a towel to soak up the flow and collect the various items needed to repair the damage. This is always a precision operation involving, for example, washing, careful drying and antiseptic wipes. Luckily, I was successful quite quickly and turned my attention to the problem of how to deal with wet clothes and sleeping-bag. What on earth was I to do? To my surprise and immense relief I discovered that the disconnection could only just have happened in the struggle for position and there was virtually no wetness anywhere. Gareth and I felt like weeping at this deliverance and again settled for a few hours. I have no idea if anyone else was awake, having kept my frantic utterances to a whisper, but if so, it would have been very awkward to offer assistance.

The events of the previous day and this night must rank amongst my worst experiences in the long years since the accident. The struggles of the last half hour had a quality of desperation not often reached. I was facing problems beyond my physical capability and I was fairly certain to cause a recurrence of an old back injury. If so, how could I nurse Gareth on my own for the rest of the holiday? I was not only utterly worn out but thoroughly depressed at the thought of the next two weeks. Why hadn't we accepted our new limitations and stayed at home?

At last I drifted into an uneasy sleep from which I was shortly awoken by my brother-in-law setting off to stake a claim for our trays of breakfast, having heard that Motor Rail had been known to run out of these. What I would have given for an hour's sleep, especially since, as I was allergic to wheat flour, I wouldn't be able to eat much. However, we needed to return the compartment to daytime conditions before breakfast arrived and this couldn't be a partial affair. Gareth had to be made decent, lifted across to the other bunk and propped upright. The paraphernalia of a spinally-injured person had to be hastily concealed and the baggage stored under the seats or in any tiny, available space. We had slept in most of our clothes and longed to get refreshed, so my sister set off first to queue for the washing facilities. It was a waste of time, however, as the supply of water had run out. At least the breakfast was tolerably filling for all but me, with a good supply of rolls and other bread. There was also fruit juice, coffee and the customary small packs of butter, marmalade, milk and sugar. Once the trays were taken away, we six sat trying to be cheerful, but longing for the journey to end.

As the train slowed down at the approach to Bologna, two of us joined the wheelchair, Bethan and Matthew having at intervals checked it was still there to set their father's mind at rest. It was lifted out and brought to the doorway nearest to Gareth. As before he was bundled out and thankfully lowered into the only place in which he could sit with some degree of comfort. Nothing seemed to have been damaged or removed. A lady met us, proving that contrary to expectations, the promised phone call from Calais had been made. There was by this time nothing she could do except show the others where to wait while my brother-in-law and I collected the cars. It all seemed very haphazard. Drivers selected their keys from a pile and walked through the train until they found their own cars. After a considerable time the cars started moving. I was towards the end of the queue and discovered to my horror that the underneath of the car grounded at each junction between carriages. It was not a slight touch but required considerable acceleration to get the car past these obstacles. If the wheelchair was essential to Gareth's well-being, so was the car. It was a Ford Escort that had been specially adapted to carry this particular chair, the whole combination being known as the 'Car Chair System', and it is a good, comparatively cheap, reliable method of conveying wheelchair users. Whatever happened I must not damage the car. This was a situation in which Gareth would have excelled, but he was sitting waiting and it was up to me. Two Frenchmen who were in charge shouted at me to hurry up. At first I refused to move and, using a few French phrases and more gestures, showed them the problem. They re-positioned metal blocks at some of the junctions, but for the most part just continued shouting and waved furiously. By the time I emerged into the crowds waiting for their cars and drivers, I was in quite a state. We couldn't check the underneath of our Ford, so only time would tell if it had been damaged.

So this was the relaxing journey intended to reduce the strain of driving through France! We thankfully left the station and I did manage to re-master driving on the 'wrong' side of the road, helped by following in the wake of my brother-in-law. I was, however, too physically and emotionally exhausted to feel any confidence in our survival. What a way to start a holiday – but even worse was having the return journey in mind all through our time in Tuscany. As it turned out this was no better, in fact rather worse, since the strain told and made us irritable at times. It cannot truly be said that, when we reached home, we felt any better for our break – the horrors of the journey saw to that.

Gareth wrote a lengthy, detailed letter of complaint to Motor Rail and was assured in a reply months later that it was perfectly accessible for wheelchair passengers. There seemed nothing more for us to say.

3
Deterioration

It was Monday, only the third day since the crash, but already we were becoming accustomed to living within the confines of disaster. Bethan, Matthew and I had spent Sunday night taking it in turns to watch beside Gareth who was in more or less constant, severe pain. In one of the short, rather better, interludes he managed to make it clear to me that he was absolutely determined Matthew should not miss Villiers Park, even though it meant I would have to leave the hospital long enough to get to Swansea for clothes and other necessities. I couldn't bring myself to promise I would go, but referred to the judgement of the consultant who at long last would be seeing Gareth this morning.

Throughout the weekend we had all been worrying whether he would get the best possible treatment in CRI. We were prepared to do anything, just anything, to maximise the chances of recovery. The only member of the extended family to have a medical career was a cousin who was a consultant in a London hospital, though his expertise was in a different field. So great was our need, that, quite against avowed egalitarian principles, we wondered if there was any way in which he might use his influence in Gareth's favour. However when I was able to speak to him on the phone, my cousin told me that the consultant he assumed we would see was a professor and an acknowledged expert in spinal injury. Nobody would be better. Immediately we gave up all vague plans of a dramatic dash to reach a 'miracle worker' – there was no more sensible alternative course of action than to wait and hope.

Early in the morning Matthew and I joined Bethan, who was on the last night-shift, and the whole family eagerly anticipated the consultant's crucial visit. We watched the frenetic activity of the nurses as they engineered two rows of 'squeaky clean' patients covered with neatly smoothed and cornered sheets in a startlingly spruced up, aseptic ward. After much discussion we decided that Bethan and Matthew should beat a strategic retreat at the last minute whilst I stayed to give Gareth support as he faced the great man. How the time dragged – it was well past ten before we saw the consultant with his substantial, deferential retinue enter. Our feverish anticipation rose dramatically, but soon abated as he set off down the other side of the ward. Gareth would be the last patient to be seen.

It must have been an hour later that a nurse drew the curtains around the bed in readiness. Bethan and Matthew vanished. I do not think that at any time during this sorry story I felt greater misery than now. My protection of the other three from the news that would devastate them must surely end. This professor would doubtless reveal the worst in as brusque a manner as the underling of yesterday. Once Gareth knew that he would never recover, there would be no hiding it from the others. We waited another ten minutes, then through the curtains held apart by the staff nurse came a rather small, quite elderly man having all the aura of importance suitable to his position.

The retinue humbly shuffled into place around the bed so that the small curtained area seemed very over-populated. I stood nervously to attention near Gareth's head, hoping nothing had been said of my making a nuisance of myself by demanding to see an expert on a Sunday. The consultant introduced himself civilly to Gareth as Professor Blain, already showing himself to be an improvement on the registrar of yesterday. Apart from an initial cursory nod in my direction he ignored me – and indeed judging from my lifelong experience of hospitals many practitioners will only address the patient. (This was spectacularly true of a rude but able consultant when examining my then three-year-old daughter's weak eyes.) I was glad to remain silent since I was completely demoralised and Gareth at this stage was not only avid for information but also able to speak. He would cope – that is until he had been told he would never walk again.

I cannot pretend that Professor Blain was friendly. He was distant, dignified and slightly forbidding. But he was 'civilised' and capable of speaking to patients more or less as human beings. He showed no particular empathy with Gareth's situation yet was informative in a neutral, professional manner. We were grateful for what was offered, only later being shown that genuine sympathy and friendliness were possible in senior staff – in regular visits from his specialist senior registrar, Mr Wood. Today he was second in the sombre procession and was necessarily silent in the presence of his superior. However on many other occasions he would draw up a chair, straddle it facing its back and chat as well as advise – in a few minutes raising the spirits not only of Gareth but the whole family.

In substance Professor Blain confirmed what we had been told at Glangwili. The break in the bone was not in itself the problem since it would heal in about six weeks if held in position – but the crux of the matter was whether the nerves would be able to follow their old pathways once the inevitable bruising and swelling subsided. Gareth breathlessly (literally and metaphorically) pressed Professor Blain for a prediction as to whether he would recover. The reply was guarded, 'There is a small chance you will make a complete recovery and there is a rather bigger chance there will be some improvement – but both probabilities will decrease over time.' Motionless by Gareth's pillow I struggled to keep tears of relief pouring down my face. There was, there really was, some chance that he would get better, whatever had been said yesterday by the duty registrar and assumed by the nurse! I had lived for twenty-four hours with the secret certainty of permanent paralysis and now to have some degree of hope! Gareth was continuing to demand precise percentages for his hope of recovery. I believe twenty and fifty per cent were mentioned, but since I did not write the figures down, can't be sure. All his browbeating failed to produce any further degree of certainty – indeed we knew perfectly well that it is impossible to predict from general probabilities to individual cases – yet since all our hopes of future happiness depended on the answer to that question, he had to keep on asking. We had to be satisfied with the knowledge that disaster was not inevitable. This was enough to make me ecstatic, for of course, even with the slightest of chances, I just knew Gareth would be lucky!

Professor Blain now embarked on a detailed explanation of how the position of the break along the spine determines fairly precisely the remaining capability for movement in the patient. In a way we didn't want to hear this – it would only become importantly relevant if Gareth failed to recover. However, though I am not very clear about this, he went on to tell us that if someone has the exact range of movement normally associated with a particular break, his injury is described as 'complete'. If there are any significant anomalies, the break is 'incomplete'. Gareth's break was between the C6 and C7 vertebrae (the C stands for cervical.) This usually leaves the victim completely paralysed below mid-chest level, but with fairly good arm and neck movement, sufficient muscles to allow for the possibility of breathing without assistance, and wrist extension. The latter meant nothing to us at the time, but we soon learnt that it is the ability to control the angle of the hand in relation to the arm. The next higher break, C5/6, usually results in a strongly characteristic positioning of the hands, namely turning out at the wrists and with the tops of the fingers tightly curled around. I think Mr Blain was meaning to be encouraging, in effect saying, 'you could be worse!' but at the time we could hardly grasp the implications of all this.

Gareth had been trying all along to raise the other vital question which obsessed us. Pausing often to snatch enough breath to continue, he said, 'Because I've had ankylosing spondylitis since I was nineteen, my neck was fused at an unusual angle. Now it's been set in a more upright position, so the nerves won't be able to find their old paths, will they? Shouldn't it be put back exactly where it was for the best chance of recovery?' Professor Blain thought for a moment before saying, 'It's unlikely a change of neck angle will make any difference.' I was far from happy with this response. I wanted a reason for this judgement, something scientific, as a ground for hope. 'Unlikely' seemed vague and unsatisfactory. Once again Gareth tried to press for more encouraging information, but without success. Quite soon the professor uttered a rather formal farewell and led his procession from the ward. He had been almost half an hour with us.

I hastened to draw back the curtains around the bed and an anxious Bethan and Matthew burst out from the patients' withdrawal room, the door of which they had kept ajar. Very quickly we gave them the gist of the expert's words and they were young enough to be optimistic – as long as there was some chance of recovery, surely their father would be one of the lucky ones! Listening to their cheerful talk and seeing the effect on Gareth, I was profoundly grateful that I had not repeated the dire prediction of the Sunday's duty registrar. Now I was able to give the full story of that interview and revelled in the family's lively denunciation of that man. Also I was able for the first time to form a clearer view of what had happened then. It occurred to me that he had more or less certainly not bothered to look at Gareth's 'notes', and that he was not a spinal injury specialist. As for his pretending reluctance to keep the truth from Gareth, I could now see that he had not intended to do anything at all beyond shutting me up, let alone speak to the patient! His sole aim was to get back to whatever he was enjoying before the rude interruption.

I had asked Professor Blain if it was safe for me to leave Gareth for some hours as there were many things I needed to sort out at home. More positive about this than anything else, he said there was nothing I could do to help at present, and that anyway Gareth's condition was not causing concern. Bethan undertook the task of keeping her father entertained and as cheerful as possible. We were as a family nearer to happiness than at any time since the accident, but were all too aware of the fragility of this mood.

It was so hard to leave the hospital, but grimly Matthew and I took a taxi to the station, a train to Swansea and another taxi home. As I put the key in the lock, the magnitude of what had happened since we were here last overwhelmed me and I suspect Matthew was feeling much the same. However we were cheered by a very affectionate welcome from our cat who was not used to being deserted like this. Matthew told me to forget about his packing and with his usual efficiency was ready long before I had finished making several vital phone calls.

The trouble was that I was hindered by in-coming calls. Family, friends and colleagues were desperately trying to find out either what had happened to us all or, if they had heard about the accident, how Gareth was. Some neighbours appeared at the door having been very worried about the disappearance of the whole family in term-time. Apart from making arrangements to feed our cat and contacting close relatives, I had not previously thought of letting people know what had happened, being wholly wrapped up in the situation at the hospital – so the spread of the news was very haphazard. Earlier this morning I had let my school know I would not be in for at least a week. Our friends who were at the scene of the accident would certainly have informed the university of what had happened and told them not to expect Gareth for a long time. No sooner did I replace the receiver than another ring would herald the commiserations of one more upset caller. Each needed time to come to terms with what they heard.

I sat in the study with Snowy purring at my feet and began to follow the instructions Gareth had given me for Saturday morning. To start with I had to arrange to get the wrecked car to 'Lakeside Honda', our usual garage. First I rang Ammanford police to find out where the car was. This proved to be difficult. Indeed we were soon into the realms of Feydeau farce. Having given them the time, date and location of the accident, I told them that the police had attended and, presumably, had arranged for the car to be towed away. Naturally I thought this an absolutely simple enquiry, but for some reason the records of Friday evening were not now available. I believe they said that everything was transferred on computer to Carmarthen at the end of the week. However they undertook to find the car. I was asked to wait and heard someone call out with a strong Welsh accent and in a relaxed tone of voice, 'That accident at Golden Grove on Friday – anyone know where they took the car? Who was on duty?' This seemed a little quaint as a way of recovering official information and, in less fraught circumstances I may have seen the funny side of it. I caught distant voices answering. After a little time I was told that the person who they thought had attended the accident (the speaker did not seem very sure who it was), was not on duty now. There was no mention of trying to contact him; rather they promised to ring around all the local garages that took in crashed cars for the police and ask each one if they had our Honda. They would ring me back. Again this seemed an astonishing way to proceed and I was getting impatient, thinking of

Bethan coping on her own. Eventually the police did ring back with the name of a garage, its address and telephone number. Thankfully I rang the AA. They were surprisingly unhelpful, saying I had not given enough information for them to be able to collect the car. Though I had repeated the name, address and phone number of the garage and said it was on the main road between Llandeilo and Carmarthen, they also needed the number of the road. It was then I rang the garage and found they knew nothing of an accident and certainly did not have the car.

This was getting beyond a joke. In despair I contacted the Ammanford police again and later they claimed once more to have found the car and gave me a telephone number. When I rang this there was no answer. Apart from ringing Lakeside Honda, who agreed immediately to accept the car, should it ever be found, I felt this particular problem would have to be shelved. My frustration was building and building as I thought of Gareth worrying over the car – as if he didn't have enough on his mind!

Thankfully I was more successful in my contacts with our solicitor. He was about to go on holiday but gave the name of his partner who in fact contacted us at the hospital later that day. Finally I rang Hourmont Holidays, cancelling our family trip to Turkey arranged for the following week. They were very sympathetic and said we would have a full refund, which indeed we received in a remarkably short time. Grabbing some clothes for Bethan and myself, we started the return journey. Matthew was very much aware of my desperation, sharing it himself, and kindly sorted out some food for us to eat on the train

– I would never have bothered on my own. We had been longer than anticipated and the thought of what was happening in the hospital was unbearable.

Bethan was overjoyed to see us. I suspected she had found our absence long, since Gareth's condition seemed to have deteriorated and she had spent several hours watching and coping. I felt unutterably sad that she had gone through all this. He was in constant pain and felt dreadfully sick. He was given anti-sickness tablets but felt no better. In fact the pressure on his chest increased and he found it more and more difficult to breathe. He was not able to eat, and drank nothing except the occasional sip of water we constantly offered. However, somehow or other he managed to convey to Matthew once again his determination that Villiers Park was not to be missed. Bethan, too, needed to be away the next day. She had just graduated, and there were various arrangements to be made with the English department at Bristol University about her degree ceremony. Having sorted out these plans for the morrow, Bethan and I returned quite late to our room for some sleep. Matthew stayed until I returned after a few hours. Before I left her, I tried to persuade Bethan after her stressful day to let me stay with Gareth until morning. It was a terrible night. I watched him struggling for breath, in pain and utter misery, hour after hour. He hardly slept at all in spite of sleeping tablets. I hoped Bethan in her exhaustion would not wake, but just as I thought I could bear it no more, she appeared. We watched together for a while until finally she made me get some rest.

The next morning began fairly well. Gareth seemed more comfortable and brighter, so quite cheerfully we saw Bethan depart for Bristol. Matthew was soon packed ready for Oxford. He was not actually leaving until a taxi would collect him at about half-past three. I was hoping that Gareth would seem to be progressing well so that Matt would have a reasonably optimistic picture to take with him. However, by early afternoon his father was again struggling for breath and was worse than at any time up to the present. The pulse-oxymeter alarm blared frequently. Sometimes this machine, which signalled too little oxygen in the blood, was merely triggered by the finger connection slipping off, whereupon we hastened to replace it. Sometimes earlier, asking Gareth to take some deep breaths would stop the alarm, showing the oxygen level had risen to an acceptable level. This stratagem produced no real relief now. Matthew and I sat on either side of the bed, pale with horror, and I could read in Matt's face how he was suffering. The three of us were getting terribly tense, especially Gareth who thought each breath was his last. From time to time I asked Janet, on duty again and very busy, to look at him. She grew increasingly worried and eventually sent for a doctor. X-rays were taken and showed that the bronchial tubes were highly congested.

About the same time it was also noticed that Gareth's bowels had not opened since the accident so the stomach was distended, and added to the pressure on the lungs. It was decided that a tube needed to be fitted through his nose and passed down the throat to the stomach so that the 'gunge' could be removed and he could be fed more easily. As far as I remember, but do not really understand how it worked, the same tube was used for both functions – maybe there were in fact two tubes. Then followed an episode which Gareth remembers with particular horror to this day. Luckily for us Matthew and I were sent away and the curtains were drawn around the bed, so we did not witness this distressing scene. Whether his nasal passages are unusually small or for some other reason, it was very difficult to thread the tube through the nose. It took three attempts, the last and successful one effected by a hastily-summoned expert in inserting such tubes in the noses of the elderly. Gareth's throat became really painful and he constantly retched in an instinctive reaction to remove the foreign body at the back of his mouth. The tube, held in place by sticking plaster, added to the bulky collar and oxygen mask to make him almost unrecognisable. However, a litre of green fluid quickly drained through the tube and thereafter a constant flow was maintained. The pressure on Gareth's chest was greatly relieved and he could breathe much more easily.

Matthew was able to leave his father obviously feeling so much better, a fact which pleased me enormously. I knew all too well how he would worry in any case. He thought I would protect him from the worst when he rang from Oxford, so I had to make serious promises to tell the truth, however bad. Since in those days we had no mobile phone, we had to make precise arrangements about when to ring. Then he said goodbye and I waved him off in his taxi. When Bethan returned she found Gareth breathing easily and feeling happier. The easing of this terrible pain made us quite light-headed with relief and, temporarily at least, we ignored possible, even probable, future misery. Gareth would get completely better and we would live as before.

We three all assumed that Gareth would have a good

night, especially since he had been given an injection as well as sleeping tablets to dull the pain. We were wrong. He fell into a shallow, disturbed sleep. His collar, yet another new one, was very uncomfortable and again there were raw places where it touched areas on which the head rested. But now the most worrying aspect of his condition was that, for the first time, he was delirious. Whether he had been given morphine and this was responsible we shall never know. Throughout the night he ran his department in the university, apparently taking part in a staff meeting. He cried out, for instance 'Who is chairing this meeting?', 'Are there any examination scripts outstanding?', 'It's not on the National Curriculum!' I remembering saying at one point, 'The only thing on the National Curriculum for you is sleep!' I was frightened by this new development and though I could calm Gareth temporarily, I did not 'get through' to him properly at all and he soon returned to his phantom world. Bethan insisted on her vigil in the early hours, though I was getting yet more worried about the effect this was having on her. When I returned to the bedside at about seven o'clock, Gareth said 'Asa Briggs [the famous historian] was brought in here in the middle of the night.' I was uncertain about how to take this and said 'I wonder what he was doing in Wales. He surely isn't Welsh?' A puzzled look came over Gareth's face and he said 'Perhaps it wasn't him but some of his books.' Gradually the drug wore off and soon he was able to smile at the various remarks he had made in the night.

This morning, Wednesday, as Gareth was still breathing easily and seemed more comfortable, I planned to rush back to Swansea for a quick, essential visit to my school.

I had been teaching the top junior class who would be leaving at the end of term in a couple of weeks' time. The headmaster had been exceptionally kind, telling me to forget school and its problems. Luckily the official business to do with progression to secondary school had been completed. However there was so much I had planned to do. Our project that term involved a study of the Victorians and we had almost completed a model of the 'Crystal Palace'. Also we were about to embark on making a series of Victorian toys that we had already researched. In science there was work to be completed on the human skeleton and, in line with our novel-based approach to language, the most exciting and valuable exercises on the last chapters remained to be tackled. I was sorry that the children would be missing these and many other activities. I had become very attached to my class and was trying to make the big transition easy for them as well as filling their last weeks in primary school with interest and enjoyment.

My main reason for feeling that I should call in the school was to do with the 'leavers' concert, always performed in front of parents and the rest of the school. I had stimulated my class to discuss and then write down their most significant memories of their time in school. They had responded magnificently and we intended to act out a few scenes from each year. This was potentially such fun, especially since each teacher would be acted by a child! Bethan and I had worked on the script in odd moments since the accident. Also we made up light-hearted words, based on the children's ideas, about different aspects of their school life set to well-known tunes. For instance, I remember there was a song for the rugby boys to sing about matches won and lost, and notable events and characters. They were to perform this with linked arms and high-kicking legs to the tune of 'Match of the Day'! We had to shelve the more serious instrumental items since I could not be there for rehearsals. I needed to drop the script at school and organise group practices of the different scenes in my absence. This final extravaganza meant a lot to my pupils, and if at all possible, I would not let them down. The problem was leaving poor Bethan in charge of Gareth again after her dreadful experience on Monday. When the consultant came on his rounds, he was reasonably satisfied with Gareth and thought the breathing problem had been solved with the use of the nasal tube. He saw no difficulty in my plan to pay a flying visit to Swansea. Bethan and Gareth were in full agreement so off I rushed.

My welcome at school nearly reduced me to tears. The children were lining up in the playground after break as I stepped out of the taxi. I heard delighted shouts of 'Here's Mrs Jones!' As I crossed to the demountable which housed my class, many tumbled down the steps to greet me. I was touched when one particularly troublesome boy held the door open and offered to carry my books. When eventually restored to order in their seats, they looked at me with solemn faces which clearly showed how deeply they sympathised, although but ten years old. It was hard to talk normally, but as we read through the parts for the concert and shared a laugh at the words of the songs, the atmosphere lifted to an almost familial closeness. They promised to learn everything and I said I would do my level best to come the following week for the actual concert. (In the event Bethan came to the school twice to take rehearsals as I wouldn't leave Gareth. Matthew and I did get to the actual performance.) As I was leaving I was given a folder containing limericks which every child had written and illustrated for 'Mr Jones'. I was instructed to read them to him to 'cheer him up'.

I called in the staff room, empty except for our nursery nurse. She was very understanding and suddenly, I suppose in reaction to my emotional reception, I found myself unable to speak and turned away to conceal my distress. A few minutes saw me gain some self control, thank the headmaster for all his support and set off home in another taxi. I needed to collect some essentials for the coming week. Not an hour had elapsed since I had reached school, but as I entered the house the phone rang. It was Bethan clearly attempting to conceal desperation. She said that Gareth's breathing was much worse and begged me to get back as soon as possible. I heard tears in her voice – she who had struggled so manfully to hide her feelings for my sake. Obviously I had made the wrong decision and should have ignored my professional responsibilities. I knew at once there had been some awful development. Dashing out of the house in panic, I would not waste time waiting for a taxi but drove my Metro to the station, abandoning it in the car park in complete indifference to what might become of it. I must get back to the hospital at all costs.

Interlude

Dependence

'I'll be absolutely fine on my own. You won't be long and are only a few hundred yards away. Go now or you'll be late.' Scarcely half an hour had elapsed when the phone rang in the through-lounge and, with it, the realisation that it hadn't been switched over from the extension in the study. It is always impossible not to think a vital message will be lost if it stops ringing before it is answered, in this case resulting in a hurried wheelchair journey into a dark room. The wheelchair footplate crashed into the door frame, somehow dislodging a foot, which got jammed between a wheel and the floor. With no feeling in the foot to show what had happened, the chair continued for another yard or two. There was a curious restriction in the driving – something was horribly wrong. The violent headache, presaging the dangerous condition of autonomic dysreflexia, would surely start. Naturally the phone had stopped ringing and was out of reach . . .

Without first hand experience it is impossible for anyone to grasp the full meaning of dependence. Not so many years ago, someone with Gareth's level of spinal injury would have been able to do almost nothing themselves. Thanks to many medical and technical advances, alternative procedures for the disabled have been developed to make everyday activities, such as eating, writing or even driving, possible. In fact the resulting life may seem from the outside to approach normality, yet the dependency, albeit less, remains. By describing some aspects of our daily life, I hope to give some indication of what such dependency means to Gareth and other disabled people – to show perhaps some of the biggest frustrations.

Probably the worst part of the day is the twenty minutes or half an hour it takes to get Gareth into bed. He will have enjoyed his favourite snack of Ryvita and cheese with a small glass of wine, while watching a news programme on television. I will have relaxed in the bath reading one of a selection of light novels kept for this purpose. At about eleven o'clock he drives into the bedroom and parks the chair between the two beds. I present him with an electric toothbrush already smeared with paste, taking care not to switch it on until it's in his mouth or we get splattered with white specks. He can control this well, holding the thick handle between his unyielding fingers. Next I administer some eye-drops, before removing the clothing from his upper body. We have a ceiling hoist which lifts Gareth up from the chair, takes him across the room and lowers him on to the bed, all electrically operated by a hand control. The only effort required is getting the nylon sling in position underneath him, especially in pulling it sideways under the lifeless legs. There are four loops in this which need to be attached correctly to the hoist or he would fall to the floor. Then the remainder of his clothing needs to be removed, the nylon sling pulled from under him, a pillow placed between his legs to prevent sores where the skin would touch, and special slippers put on for the same reason. Then I turn him onto his side, attach the night drainage bag and position the duvet and head-pillow. Finally there is the alarm clock to set and clothes to be put out ready for the morning district nurse. Really there isn't so very much to do, and mostly it seems to happen automatically while we talk. But we are both tired by now. My back is likely to be hurting and Gareth suffering from various kinds of discomfort or pain. If there is an altercation during the day, it's likely to be now – starting from the merest trifle.

Gareth spends the night in a much-hated, single, hospital bed. If the district nurses were to carry out their ministrations with him in a double bed, it would require more physical effort thus increasing their chance of injury. There is a hard, plastic-covered mattress resting on a heavy metal frame which can be electrically raised, again to make nursing easier. A second corrugated, 'Spenco' mattress is supposed to help prevent bedsores. There has been a huge amount of research into the development of ways to change automatically the areas of skin taking the weight of the prone body. We've tried several of these 'advanced' mattresses, for instance, one which gradually tilted from side to side, taking two hours to complete the process fully. In theory, the patient should be slowly turned from side to side, but Gareth's knees were so rigidly bent that he was in danger of slipping off the bed. Another had electrically operated panels which rose and fell, thus changing pressure points. To cut a very long story short, none has made any real difference to Gareth and, since he has the type of skin most susceptible to pressure sores, he will always need to be manually turned in the middle of the night.

A second major area of research has been into the easiest way to turn a patient. An increasing awareness of the amount of back trouble experienced by nurses has been largely responsible for this. For a long time we used a sleeping-bag-shaped slippery sheet, though Gareth lay on, not in, it. On top of this we had a second nylon sheet with handles sewn into the sides. The function of the under sheet was to ease the movement of the upper one. Recently we've been provided with two even more slippery sheets, which move against each other with virtually no friction – a great improvement, though, ideally, they should be a more convenient shape, shorter and narrower.

What is so astonishing to a 'normal' person is that, once arranged, Gareth can't move for the next four hours or so. This is why all the preparations are important. If, for instance, he happened by accident to be lying on something hard, or worse still, sharp, the skin could be damaged in a way that could take months to heal. He wouldn't feel anything at all below the uppermost chest level. It is ironic that as his shoulders get stiff from being in one position for so long, Gareth's only true sensation is often one of pain.

Occasionally he has violent muscular spasms which contort the whole body and catch his breath. Virtually always he has a tremendously strong burning sensation in his legs, though they are usually in fact ice-cold to the touch due to poor circulation. Worst of all he gets awful nerve-root pains. Since the nerves below the break are not functioning properly, any physical malfunction, such as indigestion or inflammation of the skin, as well as more serious problems, results in the pain being re-routed to the hands. This can be agonising, and more or less protracted and frequent. Sometimes it's virtually continuous and we can neither trace a cause nor make it any better.

Luckily, Gareth, miraculously after such a physically static day, can usually sleep quite well for much of the night if these problems are not severe. He tries not to wake me before the four-thirty alarm, since he knows I never get a long or undisturbed night. Sometimes he's been lying awake in discomfort or pain, listening for the grandfather clock in the through-lounge to strike the hour. I beg him to rouse me to change his position or give him a drink should this happen, but he won't unless absolutely desperate. Also, unfortunately, we are both inclined to be kept awake by worrying, particularly about Bethan and Matthew, often with little or imagined cause. Gareth sometimes becomes obsessed with things which have inflated importance in his present state, such as faults with his voice-operated computer, his wheelchair or the car. Our whole attitude to the world has changed with the realisation there is no such thing as a 'charmed life', that no-one is ultimately protected from the worst that life can offer.

If we are lucky, the first sound we hear in the morning is that of our alarm clock playing the music of 'Cuckoo, cuckoo, let's dance to a merry tune', followed by an American voice saying, 'Now don't be angry. It is seven o'clock precisely and you did ask me to wake you!' Revolting as this is, at least the combination of speech and music has never failed to wake one of us. I'm not sure if it is marginally better or worse than the middle-of-the-night awakening when I turn Gareth to his other side. At least in the latter case there is the delightful subsiding into bed for a further two and a half hours. I started this paragraph 'If we are lucky . . .' More often than not I'm awoken by a sharp intake of breath, the sound of a strong muscular spasm, or even a groan. Then, the first thing I am conscious of is that Gareth is in pain. Quite obviously he's the one that is suffering, but I must say that, for me, watching and hearing this is the hardest part to bear of the whole miserable situation.

Once I stagger out of bed, my first action, on alternate days, is to turn Gareth on to his back so that his legs, by their own weight, will lie almost straight and flat. He doesn't find this position very comfortable, but it's necessary as his hips get stiff from inactivity and he could end up permanently curved. On the remaining alternate days I start some medical procedures at seven o'clock so as to be ready by the time the district nurse arrives. Meanwhile I wash, get dressed, breakfast and organise the house for the day. Gareth can only lie and wait, drifting in and out of consciousness as the spasms dictate. This can be one of the most frustrating times for both of us. He longs to be up, to have breakfast and start doing something worthwhile. I am capable of getting him up and indeed do so when, for instance, he has to be anywhere fairly early or if we are away. However great the temptation is for me to do this every morning, I need to remind myself forcibly of the deterioration in my back with the onset of arthritis since the accident. Any extra strain would shorten the period in which I'm able to get Gareth in and out of bed in the afternoons, prepare him for the night and turn him in the early hours. Once I simply can't do these things – and in bleak moments we see this time just around the corner – we will really have lost our independence and have a depressingly restricted life. The only time, very early on, we relied on help for the above, the day-nurses got Gareth up from his afternoon rest at about six, whilst the night-nurses came to put him to bed before eight! Also the arrangement was that he should be turned at two o'clock in the morning – we lay awake for an hour, I turned him, we settled, and in marched two cheery nurses! So it would be difficult to plan with any degree of precision and the whole battle for a nearly normal life would have been lost for ever. Now, however, we can be very versatile within the confines of Gareth's skin routine.

So Gareth waits, getting more and more uncomfortable. During the week the nurses come between a quarter past eight and nine; at the weekends it tends to be rather later. Some of the nurses, knowing Gareth's desperation to get up, make a huge effort to come early, often attending to him before going to their headquarters to find out the rest of their work. We couldn't be more grateful for such kindness. The weekend nurses are of a grade which means they are unable to deal with one of the regular medical tasks, so I, with no nursing training of any sort, do this. Recently there has been a change in Gareth's weekday care, so healthcare support workers alternate with fully trained district nurses. Sometimes, if there has been a delay and Gareth is very uncomfortable, I cannot resist starting the washing and dressing.

One of our greatest worries is that someone in authority will attempt to cut further the amount of expert professional care which Gareth needs. Indeed, there have been disquieting hints in this direction as community nursing budgets seem to have been remorselessly squeezed, despite the enormous injections of money which have ostensibly been earmarked for the health service recently. It does not seem unreasonable that the state should be prepared to invest in an hour of daily care when I have sole responsibility for the remaining twenty three. By now I have become fairly competent in the physical aspects of caring for Gareth and am able to do the routine activities when he is in a stable condition. However, I am certain that I have neither the expertise nor the physical strength to have sole responsibility for him. His delicate skin needs constant, expert observation. There are also so many questions about the significance of ailments which aren't serious for most people – the common cold, for example, needs to be monitored so that it doesn't develop into a chest infection which may easily become pneumonia. We are both grateful to be able to turn to nurses who have been trained to cope with immobile people and give us reassurance and advice. It is also a great relief for me to have some respite from the lifting and turning which have helped develop an arthritic hip and muscular problems in both legs.

The nurses are cheerful and kindly, very often more like friends than people doing a job. But, however pleasant they are, it is no enviable position that Gareth is in. (I have heard youngsters in hospital saying to the injured people they are visiting 'I wouldn't mind being nursed by her!' as they see a pretty nurse at work. Obviously they know nothing of the reality of the situation.) It can't be anything but demeaning for an adult to be washed and dressed like a baby. Gareth tries on the one hand not to think of what is happening, but on the other to check that everything is done. Once he is winched into the chair, dressing is finished and his eye-drops administered. After cleaning his teeth Gareth washes his face and hands using a mitten-shaped flannel originally brought from France. The shaver is in a special moulded holder so he can shave himself. Finally his hair is combed and he escapes in the chair to the through-lounge, only now beginning to feel 'human'.

I will have opened the post (there can no longer be any privacy here either) and put the contents in his easy reach on top of the newspaper, so he can sort the former, then start reading the latter, while he eats. We don't have a 'civilised' breakfast together since I have been up for hours by now. Gareth can only manage a small bowl of cereal and a cup of tea, together with some tablets. He casts junk mail on to a nearby settee for me to throw away, makes a pile of the correspondence he needs to deal with and leaves the rest on the table to be read later. After I have double-checked that everything about him is safe, he drives into the study, balancing the pile of letters on his knees. There may be some administration that I need to help with; if so he directs me to file papers, or address envelopes, for instance. This is not one of my favourite activities but there is no escaping it and we usually manage to keep relatively cheerful.

At last Gareth is able to start his morning's work. This is the time of day when he feels least discomfort and can do most. First he completes the remainder, and what is undoubtedly the greater part, of the administration. He uses his voice-operated computer for faxes and e-mails. His telephone is an important part of the communication system (called 'Possum', provided by what was then the Welsh Office) which is operated from the wheelchair without having to reach a normal receiver. BT provide an excellent free information service for those unable to access a directory. When everything essential is completed, he turns to his 'real' work: namely writing articles or chapters of books, editing journals or books, and also writing lectures. He finds it difficult to undertake large-scale works that would involve much research into primary sources because of the practical problems involved in getting to them, but has achieved an amazing amount since the accident. To come upon Gareth sitting in the study, wholly wrapped up in his work, it would be easy to think that there were no particular problems involved. He seems to be completely in control – and indeed he is, unless for instance, something falls to the floor or a piece of paper, file or book is out of reach. If he is in the house on his own, hours of working time can be wasted and frustration build up.

For a long time it wasn't safe to leave Gareth at all, but now he even says that he enjoys having the house to himself for a few hours. This may or may not be entirely true, and the opening paragraph of this chapter shows that disaster is never far away. There are various safety procedures in position. He has an 'Aid-call' pendant round his neck which he could activate in extreme emergencies, though he hasn't done so yet. The organisation, oddly enough, is centred in Devon and a single touch on the pendant will cause a phone to ring at that office. We have given them a series of numbers starting with neighbours and ending with our local police. They will ring these in turn until someone promises to check up on Gareth. Apart from this he can use the Possum control, which is held by elastic bands to the arm of his wheelchair, to operate an alarm which sounds outside the front door – or indeed to ring someone. I now have a mobile phone which is always on when I am out of the house.

Obviously then, there are several things I need to do before leaving Gareth for a few hours. I give him the emergency pendant; check the key to the front door is in its hiding place; empty the leg-bag; leave a hot drink in the study and a cold one in the lounge; make sure newspapers, periodicals or books are in reach; balance the controls to the television, radio, CD and tape-recorder as usual on the back of a particular arm-chair; and ask if he has all he needs for work! When, until two years ago, I taught three afternoons a week, we had a delightful, wholly dependable lady who came to be in the house with Gareth and was a great help with the housework. Now I'm retired she only comes for one morning on a regular basis, but is always ready to help if I need to be out for long. I am very grateful to her because, in spite of the emergency arrangements, I'm never wholly at ease when I know he is on his own. Now that ten years have passed since the accident, I don't expect this tension to slacken. I seldom dally on my expeditions, breathing a sigh of relief that all is well when I get home.

We have gradually pieced together a lifestyle in which Gareth has a kind of fragile, temporary independence. Quite unaided, he continues with his mostly unpaid academic work, moves freely around the downstairs of our home, answers the door and the phone, operates the television, radio and hi-fi, reads widely and enjoys a ready-prepared snack – you might almost say 'like the old days'. Yet none of this is possible if not planned with, and organised by, someone else. A shut door, an obstacle on the floor in the path of the chair, something just out of reach, and a thousand other things can cause disruption. For instance, tipping a hot drink, a power cut or violent spasms can be major disasters.

It is not true to say that Gareth accepts his dependence. The infinite number of frustrations, some small, some vast, that make up most of his day will ensure that. Having to ask people constantly to do things for him is also very difficult, regardless of whether he knows they are quite happy to help. Yet, in spite of everything, he doesn't spend much of his time rebelling against his lot. Within all the limits and restrictions he presses on with what he does best.

4

Intensive Care

The London train was due in five minutes and I was almost tearfully grateful for this stroke of luck. At Cardiff I ran for a taxi and arrived at the hospital in the shortest possible time. It had seemed long to me and, I soon discovered, infinitely longer to Bethan. Ten years later I can hardly bear the burden of my responsibility for what she suffered that afternoon. Soon after mid-day Gareth's breathing had become laboured, the alarm on the pulse-oxymeter sounded at frequent intervals and pressure on his chest increased rapidly. Bethan had called a nurse who had obviously been worried. Two doctors appeared, more X-rays were taken and a physiotherapist tried to help his breathing. Curtains were drawn around the bed. Outside, Bethan listened to all the urgent activity and became convinced that her father was going to die. She waited in desperation for me to appear. One of the doctors came from behind the curtain to explain to her that Gareth might have to be taken into Intensive Care. He could then be fitted with a more effective oxygen mask and, if this failed, a ventilator would help him breathe. Bethan felt his death seemed even more certain and all she could pray for was that I would get back before it happened.

As I rushed into the ward, I caught a glimpse of Bethan standing alone outside the drawn curtains looking hopelessly towards the door. Her face lit up and we hugged each other as I asked urgently what had happened. Beths, with tremendous courage, tried to sound positive for my sake, but when we both peered through the curtains, I instantly grasped the bleak truth. Gareth looked dreadful and was clearly struggling for each breath. Several people were busy round his bed. I tried to let him know that I was back but he was far beyond giving any signal of recognition. Even then he was being prepared for Intensive Care – the very word was enough to instil terror into the pair of us. I was only just in time to take from Bethan the crushing responsibility she felt as the only member of the family present. In a few minutes we were following as the bed was wheeled the very short distance to Intensive Care. We were asked to wait in a small triangular room just outside the door, the furniture of which had been donated by Maskreys. (I do not know how many times in vacant moments we read the plaque announcing this in the following weeks.) Gareth disappeared through large doors which closed firmly behind him. We hated being shut out and feared the worst.

Bethan went to our room for a few minutes but soon rejoined me looking terribly exhausted and sad. We saw Gareth's 'Thomas Andrew' bed being wheeled away – then nothing. This has to be counted amongst the blackest of times. Neither of us could use the usual comforting ploy of reference to Professor Blain's predictions. If Gareth couldn't even breathe, how could he live, paralysed or not? After what seemed ages one of the three senior men in charge of IC appeared and sat with us in the waiting room, taking time to give much needed reassurance. To begin with he, Dr Franklin, said Gareth was ‘comfortable’ and we weren’t to worry. Then he explained that it was not unusual for spinally-injured people to have breathing difficulties, that Gareth had a chest infection and would need more help than the mask fitted in Thomas Andrew could provide until the lungs were clear. He made us understand that the infection was simply an unfortunate additional problem which complicated the treatment of the broken neck – but we were assured it could be cured. We were told that ventilators were only used when other treatments failed and then for the shortest possible time, so that the lungs did not become too used to the extra support and unable to cope independently. Dr Franklin was wonderfully sympathetic, giving us insight into the situation and telling the truth in the least hurtful manner. He saw the gentle handling of distressed relatives of patients as an important part of his job. For Bethan and myself, he certainly lifted the worst of our despair. We began timidly to hope that at least Gareth would survive – paralysed perhaps – but alive.

A nurse came to tell us we could now go into IC. She tried to prepare us for what we would see, saying that some relatives became frightened by the vast array of machines and equipment around and attached to their loved one. Bethan and I braced ourselves to face whatever awful things lay ahead. I glanced at her and we exchanged supportive, if strained, looks. The nurse led us straight to Gareth.

Our first experience of Intensive Care was daunting. It was indeed bad enough seeing the huge collection of machines surrounding him to which different parts of his body (even his feet) were attached by lines and tubes.

Some were pushed under the skin and taped into position, others were on the surface of the body. There was also at least one drip going into his arm as well as the tube passing through his nose to his stomach, used to regulate food intake. A strong pain-killer, probably morphine, was automatically injected from a machine at regular intervals throughout the day and night. I remember counting up to thirty attachments at one time. Worst of all was a huge oxygen mask clamped firmly over Gareth's face. Bethan and I stared down at this almost unrecognisable person and saw with utter dismay that he was not only conscious but was struggling to tell us something. His eyes moved about restlessly and his mouth tried to shape words. The tight mask prevented any sound emerging but there was no doubt he was in agony. For the first time he was completely unable to communicate with us and, desperately, we sought to improvise a system that would let us find out what in particular was the matter. 'Are you feeling sick? Is the collar hurting? Is it your chest? Move your hand when we hit on the problem.' There were so many things that could be causing pain and, as far as we could tell, he didn't move his hand in response to any of our questions. He started to pull feebly at the mask (much, much later we learnt that he had panicked at the pressure of this) and we were afraid he would disturb some of the lines. We were indeed in constant terror of the latter as it was very difficult to find an unsullied area of Gareth's skin to touch and any movement round the bed or patient was hazardous.

There was only one nurse on duty at the time and though all the six or eight patients were desperately ill, they lay immobile and mostly unconscious, so it was quiet. Everything was clean and ordered, a neutral, passionless presentation of people at death's door. But Bethan and I grew more desperate. Where was the intensive care we expected? Gareth was in a terrible state and no one seemed to know or intend to do anything about it. We looked at the young, fair nurse sitting stolidly on a high stool in the centre of the ward, a position from which she could see all the patients. I plucked up courage to plead with her to get someone to attend to Gareth. She answered, 'It's the nurses' tea-break. They can only be disturbed for a cardiac arrest.' Bethan and I could not accept that the nurses were talking and laughing over coffee while Gareth was in torment. We grew more frantic as he grew rather worse and soon Bethan approached the nurse 'You've got to do something. He's in absolute agony!' This was no more productive than my previous effort. The nurse looked at her calmly and said, 'I'm sorry but he'll have to wait.' She seemed very displeased at our insistence and I began to be terrified of being turned out of the ward, so begged Bethan not to say anything more. I was afraid of what she might do, having heard her mutter 'I'm going to hit someone if this goes on.' It was an impossible situation. We kept on trying to understand what a suffering Gareth was struggling to tell us but didn't succeed. Somehow we survived the next quarter of an hour or so and were mightily relieved to see other nurses come towards Gareth. Again we were asked to wait outside.

Eventually another of the senior men, Dr Freidrich, came into the room. (The three specialists all had names beginning with F, oddly enough, the remaining one being Dr Foster.) Dr Freidrich was rather dour, less obviously sympathetic than Dr Franklin. He explained that the new mask had been inadequate so Gareth was being put on a ventilator. Here was yet another horror to confront, made worse by being told that some patients, though not many, actually went home attached permanently to theirs – a terrifying thought! When we were allowed back into the ward, Gareth was sleeping with a big plug-like contraption in his mouth through which oxygen was forced from a big, black, noisy machine. We watched the regular rising and falling of his upper chest and thanked God that his struggle was over – at least temporarily.

When Matthew rang at ten o'clock that evening as arranged, I had to tell him that his father had been taken into Intensive Care. It was hard to do this since, as Bethan and I knew all too well, the very term is so emotive, but he had to be able to trust me to tell him the truth or being away would be intolerable. (At some point during Gareth's stay in hospital IC became ITU – Intensive Therapy Unit – but it never changed for us.) Luckily there was no point in going into the awful details, and I could say that his father was sleeping peacefully at the time and that the ventilator made breathing much easier. He seemed to accept the information reasonably well (but then he would have done his level best to conceal his darker feelings), and I hoped his mind would be pretty fully engaged with work over the next week. All we could do was arrange when to phone the following day. I was only glad he had not experienced the day his sister had suffered, and would have given anything to have saved her that, too.

The nurse looking after Gareth persuaded us that we needed sleep, and that we could do nothing for him in any case since he would be kept sedated. She would be sitting at the foot of his bed and be in charge of him and only him for the whole night. Every movement and every breath would be monitored. (In fact, over the next few days we realised that no family visitors had stayed in the ward through the night and suspected that it was strongly discouraged, even forbidden.) Seeing he was deeply and peacefully asleep, I agreed to go. Bethan stayed for almost another hour in spite of her long ordeal. We tried to console each other when she joined me in the room, but it was in deep despair that, exhausted, we fell asleep. Bethan had shown almost superhuman strength of character, but could even her exuberant optimism fail to be lastingly damaged by such a day?

The next morning, soon after 7 am on 9 July, we woke, dressed hastily and hurried along the corridors to Intensive Care, dreading what we might find. We had already noticed that access to this ward was, for obvious reasons, by no means as free as in Thomas Andrew. A buzzer had to be pressed and permission given to enter. (At first we used this without embarrassment, but soon realised that the nurses had to leave their patients to let people in and were not pleased to do this often for visitors. We learnt to hang about outside the big doors until someone official came in or out, then sidled in with an ingratiating, questioning grin directed at the nearest nurse.) Today, however, the first morning, we sounded the buzzer boldly and eventually were allowed in to where Gareth was in a deep sleep, still free from the pain and agitation of the previous day. Bethan and I agreed that our strongest emotion was of relief. We could hope too that he was gathering strength by his rest, ready for a positive step towards recovery. Though he lay paralysed, neck encased in a large collar, unable to breathe on his own, attached to many complex machines and unable to communicate, we could once again cling to the words of Professor Blain – there was a chance. He was so heavily sedated that there was virtually no sign of recognition of either of us but we sat, hour after hour, sometimes whispering words of encouragement and endearment, in case, as we had been told, at some level of consciousness he heard and understood.

Gradually we became sufficiently brave to look around the ward. The other patients, all terribly ill, lay completely inert, surrounded by masses of machinery. Each had their own nurse who monitored every heart beat and breath. Occasionally some visitors sat with their relative or friend. The atmosphere, though calm, was too quiet and sombre – completely depersonalised. Everyone spoke in very hushed tones. As the morning dragged on, Bethan and I felt more and more conspicuous as permanent fixtures at Gareth's side. Sometimes we would take it in turns to get a drink, fetch a book or use the lavatory – but activated by a nagging sense of foreboding would very quickly be at the door striving for a trouble-free entry.

By lunch time Gareth was still deeply unconscious so Bethan and I decided to find our way to the staff canteen together. Since this was the first time we had used it, having each other's company would bolster our morale. We had been told when in Thomas Andrew that senior nurses could give vouchers to allow visitors to use facilities that were provided for hospital employees. It was a bit difficult to ask for these as we felt we were taking advantage in some indefinable way. However there was no other option really since we wouldn't have left the hospital for a 'proper' meal. So Bethan and I found the way up a narrow staircase to a big room full of nurses, doctors and administrators. As we gingerly edged along the counter with our trays, we saw, to our relief, that there was at least one vegetarian option. The food looked nourishing and was very cheap, no doubt heavily subsidised. We sat nervously at our table trying to eat quickly and here too feeling conspicuous, but no one seemed to think us worthy of comment. I had to struggle to swallow each mouthful, whereas Bethan seemed to find a tiny shadow of comfort in eating. In a remarkably short time we were back in the corridors thronged with medical staff and porters with their trolleys and stretchers. Here too we felt out of place, and I tried to avoid eye-contact with anyone. One pleasant doctor greeted us, but in general, we were – and wished to be – unnoticed. All we wanted was to get back to Gareth.

Bethan and I waited in frustration outside the doors of IC for about ten minutes, but at length resumed our positions on either side of Gareth's pillow. For another hour he lay unmoving, then Bethan noticed his eyes were resting on her with apparent recognition. He still couldn't as much as smile, let alone speak, but we tried to talk and laugh, anything to keep his mind off the reality of the situation. Ever since news of the accident had spread to family and friends, there had been a daily flood of letters and cards. Today an even bigger batch than usual had found their way from Thomas Andrew. An hour passed in showing these to Gareth. We read out some quite long letters, some carefully designed to be entertaining as well as offering sympathy. One of these from a colleague in

Aberystwyth was festooned with 'Chads' and we fancied a response to this humour in his eyes.

All along we confronted the problem of communication. With the ventilator plug filling his mouth and with his strength gone, Gareth's range of movement was reduced to a tiny lifting of a hand. (We had tried using blinking as a signal, but he had too little control over this.) As we had discovered on his entry to IC, this meant Bethan or I had to do the speaking, while he could only show whether he agreed. How was he to actually tell us anything? – and who knows how important a message might be to one in his precarious state? After some thought I wrote the alphabet out on a piece of paper, then pointed to each letter in turn, carefully watching that feeble hand. It was slow and frustrating, yet it worked, rather like a guessing game. 'C - A - can? - R - car! F - I - N - D - find!' I realised Gareth wanted me to repeat Saturday's abortive phone calls about the car. Leaving Bethan in charge, I set off, hoping that now, almost a week since the accident, it should be possible to dissolve Gareth's worries on this score at least.

As I needed change, I called in the kiosk selling sweets and newspapers which was on the ground floor next to the two main call boxes. To my surprise the vendor brusquely refused to change a note, saying he was asked so often that he had made it a rule not to help anyone. I tried to work out which small purchase would generate the maximum amount of suitable coins, but even then he wouldn't cooperate. At last, with my money laid out in a row and my list of numbers propped up awkwardly, I dialled the Honda garage. Surely they would have received the wrecked car by now, since two days ago the

AA had promised to move it immediately. I spoke to someone who knew Gareth well and had to answer urgent enquiries about his state of health before getting down to business. Then I found out that, although the insurance company's engineer had turned up at the Honda garage to assess the damage, the car still had not arrived. At once, in some annoyance, I rang the garage which, according to Ammanford police, had possession of the car. Somewhat to my surprise it was there. However, they said that the AA had turned up to collect it, but refused to tow it away since the wheels would not roll. This, the garage mechanic averred, was untrue. I could feel the situation spiralling towards complete chaos and rang the AA, demanding to know why they were unable to move a single damaged car in the course of a week.

I was obliged to give our AA number, the make and registration number of the car, the precise location of the accident, and full details as to what happened. My precious supply of coins was running out and I had to use the 'follow-on' system, putting in whole pounds at a time. (I already knew that the old, battered phone was hopelessly unreliable and probably would fail to transfer any remaining money to the next call.) I grew impatient as the data were painstakingly recorded. However this was nothing compared with my fury as I was passed on to different people twice – and had to repeat the lot both times! The final straw came when I was told that the garage had not let them collect the car because of unpaid debts! This was totally beyond my comprehension and, I am sorry to say, I rather lost control: 'My husband is lying in Intensive Care, unable to move or even speak, and he's got this extra worry about the car. We've paid

AA Relay membership for years. Is this how you operate? Three times you've promised to move it and three times you've let us down. And now this ridiculous reference to debts. How on earth could we be in debt to a garage we've never been near?' I realised I was shouting and an obviously shocked voice quickly promised to ring back very shortly – and the line went dead.

The AA did indeed ring back, no mean feat because ward phones were mainly for medical purposes, and private calls could block vital messages – while the bulky, black mobile phones for patients' use seemed either to be occupied or not plugged in. I spoke to a charming, sympathetic man, possibly reserved for difficult customers. Not only did he apologise and renew promises to collect the car instantly, but explained the riddle of the unpaid debts. It turned out that the garage owner had refused to part with the crashed car because no one had paid him the fee for collecting it from the scene of the accident. There was no way we could have anticipated such a charge, any more than we expected the bill that arrived months later from the local NHS Trust for Gareth being taken by ambulance to hospital. (If we had thought about it, I expect we would have decided that this at least was a free ride!) The AA – who ultimately sent us a handsome letter of apology – bore the brunt of my fury, but it is the police who are more likely to have been at fault. If they knew, as they must, that a charge was made by a garage collecting a car for them, why had they not either paid it or forwarded the bill to us? Or, at the most basic level of public relations, kept us informed?

Back in IC I told Gareth the improbable tale. I was sorry not to be able to say that the car was safely in

Lakeside Honda, but it did seem as if action would be taken at last. Feeling emotionally exhausted and foolish for having shouted, I felt little interest as a nurse approached: 'You've been chosen to move into the visitors' flat. It's called 'Arosfa' and is on the next floor. Here's the key and you can move into it whenever you like.' Here was something to raise our spirits – a totally unforeseen and much welcomed kindness. Soon we were exploring the two bedrooms, the bathroom and the sitting room. At one end of the latter was a table holding an electric kettle and some basic crockery. We found out that the flat had been furnished by a charity for the use of families of seriously ill patients whose homes were rather distant. We had been managing perfectly well in the tiny room, but relished the thought of having a bed each and the wherewithal to make a cup of tea. (Later we were asked to give 'Arosfa' up in favour of an elderly couple and did so gladly, but for quite a while it was a comfortable retreat from the ward.) That night, when thrown out from IC some time after eleven, Bethan and I sat in proper armchairs and sipped hot drinks while we tried to be positive about the events of the day. The future was unknowable, unthinkable; the dismal present was more than we could cope with; yet the existence of 'Arosfa' did supply a single ray of light.

The next day, Friday 10 July, was Bethan's graduation ceremony for her first Bristol degree. Gareth and I had proudly booked seats for this and had arranged to attend the special tea afterwards. We had planned to spend most of the day in Bristol, probably returning home late with Bethan. Perhaps partly because he is an academic himself, Gareth had attached immense significance to the ceremony and had long determined to be present whatever else was happening on that day. Now he was devastated that this was truly impossible. Bethan reminded him that there should be an MA ceremony the following year and that he would be fit by then, but the promise sounded hollow in the circumstances. One thing he was absolutely determined about – and he painstakingly spelled this out using our written alphabet – was that I should be at the ceremony for Bethan's sake. It was only an hour's train journey from Cardiff to Bristol and I could arrive just before it all started, see Bethan afterwards and rush back to the station. She would set off early to collect her gown and certificate, have the official photograph and meet friends.

With no suitable clothes in the hospital I had to run up to town, buy (without trying on) the first dress that seemed adequate and dash back to CRI. It was a fine morning as, arrayed in my new dress, I took a taxi to the station, leaving Gareth seemingly stable. He had been in IC for a whole day and we had learnt that the name was after all a true reflection of the treatment given (in spite of tea-breaks!) He would be safe, if unutterably sad. Everything went to plan and I was lucky enough to see Bethan on the way in. The ceremony in the Great Hall of the Wills Memorial Building was archaic and formal, yet moving for each parent witnessing the symbol of their child's success. I sat remembering the day I had driven Bethan (dressed in a highly uncharacteristic straight grey skirt and dark jacket) from Swansea for her interview. Afterwards we had sat in the sun in a pleasant area not far from the hall, eating our sandwiches and worrying about a pigeon with an injured foot. The memory was so vivid, yet it was over three years ago and now that schoolgirl was a graduate! I thought of the richness of her undergraduate days, of all the concerts in which we had watched her perform, of all the friendships she had made and of the mental stimulation she had experienced. I was glad this would continue for another year. Permeating every thought was the image of Gareth lying paralysed – how he would have revelled in the occasion and the sharing of memories.

Bethan looked lovely in academic dress and I had time to take some photographs of her outside the hall. Though rather pale, no one would have thought she was undergoing intense suffering. With great regret I left her to face the 'graduand and family' tea on her own. There were not as many of her friends staying for this as she had hoped and they seemed to be in family units. However, with her usual cheerful determination, she sent me back to Gareth knowing this was the first time he was in hospital without either of us. Who could have predicted that Bethan's graduation would have been like this?

I re-entered the hospital less than three hours after leaving and was very relieved to see that there had been no deterioration in Gareth's condition in my absence. He was still fairly heavily sedated and having the automatically-injected painkillers every few hours. However he was sufficiently alert to listen to my account of the graduation with obvious interest. When Bethan returned later, his eyes rested avidly on her face as she gave a lively, full account of her day. He was very tired and it was obvious could not get over his sadness at what he had missed.

Starting almost immediately after the accident, Gareth had a constant stream of visitors, including family, friends and neighbours, colleagues from Swansea, Aberystwyth and Cardiff, representatives from the United Reformed Church and, most importantly from my point of view, my three sisters. If anyone was allowed to see Gareth for a short time, it was very upsetting for them. Afterwards Bethan and I took it in turns to provide refreshments in the only possible, somewhat dismal, venue, the fracture clinic – where volunteers sold sandwiches, cakes and drinks. Over the traditional panacea of a hot cup of tea, voices would steady and eyes dry. Perhaps people wondered at my composure, but Bethan and I were so inured to misery by now that we only gave way in private.

Today, just as I returned from Bristol, my sister from Coventry arrived with her husband and stayed until late. I was pleased to think that we would no longer have to rely on the fracture clinic, repairing with them to 'Arosfa' when shut out from Gareth. Having grasped the set-up, next time they came armed with quantities of food and other necessities, even a pyrex container full of change for the phone. This is but one example of the continuing show of sympathy and support which did wonders for our morale.

The next day began encouragingly. The blood analyses and other tests were improving. Later Gareth got very distressed, grimacing and moving his arms in despair. Bethan and I were frantic and his nurse was concerned. Laboriously we found out that he was feeling sick and he began retching, as far as this was possible with so many of his chest muscles paralysed. There was complete misery for quarter of an hour or so, then an injection and increase of painkillers quietened him. We were becoming accustomed to seeing Gareth paralysed and unable to talk or breathe on his own, but here was a further descent into invalidity. Could he now only survive in even a marginally acceptable state when heavily doped?

It became increasingly obvious over the weekend that Gareth's need for the support of the ventilator was not going to be as short-term as had been hoped. One of the nurses told us he would need to have a tracheostomy. In this operation a hole is bored through the front of the neck and a tube is fitted through it into the windpipe. (She also said that the simplest and most effective thing would be to push a screwdriver into the neck – the jagged hole would heal more quickly!) The ventilator can be attached to this, leaving the mouth free. The biggest advantage is that, in the case of chest infection, sputum can be suctioned out through the tube. Gareth's temperature had risen and his chest 'thickened'. Clearly he had an infection and the doctors decided to start antibiotics straight away rather than wait for the result of the sputum analysis. When the latter was available, they would replace the broad-based antibiotic with one that was highly specific.

Matthew returned from Villiers Park as we faced this new worry. It was with mixed feelings that I welcomed him – after all, seventeen was young to be facing such terrible things. We had kept him informed by a daily phone call and had always told the truth, but had excluded some of the temporary upsets if they were over by the time we rang. Soon he was in the ward seeing the paraphernalia of Intensive Care and Gareth's changed condition. I watched Matthew as he took it all in, conscious of the fact that he tended to conceal his deepest feelings. Already familiar with a deadening sense of disaster, this direct experience of worsening suffering was shaking him to the core. However he did find strength to entertain his father with stories of the course which had been crammed full of musical and social activities. The rest of us smiled at the way he had so typically, in response to a challenge, stayed awake into the small hours composing an extraordinarily complex and impressive minimalist work. He showed us a glowing report written by the course director. Gareth's eyes showed his interest, but it was obvious he was in pain. Matthew struggled on with his narrative, but it began to seem forced. Soon the awfulness of the situation darkened the light Matthew had brought in from the outside world and we were in misery again.

Yet selfishly, it was wonderful to be a complete family again and now the three of us were staying in 'Arosfa' we could have more breaks from the bedside to get things done. Bethan and Matthew could go singly or together into town to buy food or whatever else was needed. For instance, the next day Matthew enjoyed choosing a battery-operated watch for Gareth since he could no longer wind his elegant gold one. He also got earphones in the hope that his father would be able to listen to the radio. But at the bedside, in spite of attempted cheer, we couldn't fool each other that there had been any improvement at all – it had been a steady downward slope – and it was impossibly hard to bear. Matthew, coming back fresh to the hospital, saw the decline even more clearly than Bethan and I myself.

Gareth had been promised the tracheostomy operation on Monday but an unexpected problem arose. The rigid collar he would need for at least six weeks until the spine fused did not have a hole in the front to accommodate the 'trache'. Measurements and X-rays were taken and storerooms searched, but no one could find a suitably designed collar that would fit Gareth. Eventually it was decided that he would have to return temporarily to the much dreaded traction. It was after five by the time this was sorted out and the four of us were weary with frustration and fear, assuming we would have to wait another day. But suddenly, while Bethan and I were having our turn to be with Gareth, two porters arrived and pushed his trolley-bed from the ward, carefully keeping the various machines attached to him in line. Bethan and I stood in the space where the bed had been, forlornly watching this complicated exit. Dr Franklin saw us, instantly understood our feelings and beckoned us into the small side room. He explained that the operation in itself was trivial, that it would make things easier and that the wound would heal of itself. As he talked we had time to get over the initial shock of seeing Gareth being wheeled away. For the second time thankful that a man in his position could be so perceptive and caring, we took his advice and returned to 'Arosfa' for a while.

By the time the bed with its attachments had passed the door of the waiting room on the way back to the ward, Matthew, Bethan and I were waiting, expecting the worst. Jumping up, we saw that Gareth was at least alive, but very yellow-looking. When we were allowed into the ward his eyes were rolled back in his head, and we could make no contact with him. His face looked curiously elongated and his dark hair was swept back oddly onto the pillow. I suppose the anaesthetic had not yet worn off, but he was a ghastly sight and we were frightened. Yet the 'trache' hole looked very neat with the 'plug' taped into position and attached to the respirator. His chest rose and fell in time with the thumps of the machine, and his face was at least clear of the mouth-tube and big collar. The pulley system and weights were once more attached to his skull, so that though he began to return to consciousness, it was to an awareness of tension through his neck and chest together with severe pains in his head. It was late by now and the family were sent to bed with half-hearted promises to phone 'Arosfa' if we were needed. Dragging ourselves wearily along the corridors, we were numb with the horror of all that had happened since the initial thunderbolt of the accident. Gareth's condition had deteriorated to such an extent that we could hardly visualise what an improvement would be like. Sipping hot drinks, we tried to comfort each other by repeating Dr Franklin's words, but though the latest ordeal had been survived, it was quite clear that there would be more.

Interlude

Italy – Caravan (1981)

Three people huddled together on the otherwise empty upper deck of a night car ferry crossing to France. The central figure had an arm around each of the smaller ones, protecting them against the vaguely menacing darkness. From this height it was easy to see the prow cutting a foaming path through the waves, the lights of passing ships and seemingly dazzling stars. The trio savoured the conflicting sensations of the hot, oily smell of the engine and the coolness of the fresh, salty air. Similarly the steady, mechanical throb mingled with the restless, unpredictable heaving of the waves. This was a close, small unit, far from land in a boundless ocean.

Below deck Gareth slept in the reclining chairs provided for longer channel crossings. He had driven to the coast from Pennard and would make inroads into the long trek south as soon as we docked. However, this was by no means his initial contribution to our holiday. Looking at his preparations, as well as his actual role during those three weeks abroad, could hardly bring out more strongly the sadness of his current condition.

It always began with the ritual of waking the caravan from its hibernation in the garden of Gareth's parents in Porthyrhyd. The tyres, which had been protected by using bricks to take the weight of the van on its axle, were now tested and inflated. Gareth then greased the 'ball' part of the ball-and-socket joint connecting the van to the car – the exposed grease was a wonderful cause of messy clothes throughout the holiday, in spite of a plastic cover used when we were parked. The car needed to be positioned accurately with the hemispherical 'socket' on the towing bracket of the van right next to the 'ball'. Surprisingly we discovered I had the knack of doing this reversing quite well, so I was called to do it, leaving the children and their grandparents to entertain each other. Gareth completed the hitch (I was often newly amazed at the simplicity yet strength of this) before plugging in the electrics with bated breath, since there was inevitably some problems due to the connections having corroded during the damp winter. At last he succeeded, but not before Bethan and Matthew had listened enchanted to the muttered 'damned electrics!'

The real moment of drama came when Gareth started the car and slowly accelerated as the mechanisms of the caravan were activated crunchingly for the first time in almost a year. After rousing cheers, all that remained was to drive out through the narrow gates right to the far side (to clear the gate) of a busy, quite dangerous road, with a great deal of enthusiastic directing from Grandpa. I was sure he would be run over, if not by passing traffic, by his son. Gareth parked at the roadside, we exchanged farewells and we were off! As we drove towards Pennard, the children kept turning round to check the van was still with us. This seemed, and in a sense was, the start of the holiday and we were happy.

During the following week Gareth meticulously serviced both van and car. Since childhood he'd been fascinated by cars, and from about the age of thirteen, had been taught basic mechanical operations by the kindly owner of a local garage in Whitland where he then lived. He was able to put these skills into practice later, as a student, when he nursed, and prolonged the life of, an old Ford 8. Over the years he serviced a Ford Consul, a series of Minis, two Renault 16s and three Honda Accords. I well remember the Christmas after he bought his first Renault, when one of his presents was the relevant complete workshop manual – and capturing his attention after this became quite a challenge! Not only was he saving substantial sums of money in looking after the cars, but he had the satisfaction of knowing that the work was done properly. Besides he thoroughly enjoyed it, in spite of, for instance, occasionally letting the engine oil drain out all over the drive by accident.

A year or two previously his preparations included installing a fridge in the van. This was much more difficult than he had anticipated, because it just wouldn't fit into the space. After struggling for days, he finally completed the job by fitting a waste gas outlet pipe to prevent us being asphyxiated, then struck a match rather nervously – and the whole thing worked perfectly! It's true that the pilot light tended to go out in transit, so one or other of us was often to be found grovelling on our knees to check it, but it was wonderful to be able to keep food cool in hot climates and Gareth was very pleased with himself.

My job was simpler, namely to clean and pack the van. Over the winter a thick, green patina had built up on the roof and walls. I used a step ladder and attacked this with stiff brush and hot, soapy water, taking care not to do the unforgivable and dent the flimsy outer surface, thus spoiling the water-proofing. The rubber channels were absolutely disgusting and I ruined several toothbrushes cleaning these. We kept the cushions used as seats and beds in a large cupboard at home, so these just needed to be hurled downstairs and placed in the van. At this stage the whole family had a ceremonial drink and biscuit sitting at the main table where we would eat, play, read and even sleep for three weeks. Any 'lucky' visitors or friends coming to play were obliged to join in.

The final stage of preparation was filling the van. Crockery, cutlery and cooking utensils were collected together with particular attention to a corkscrew and tin opener. We never really solved the wine glass problem. As a serious red wine drinker, Gareth thought it beneath his dignity to use a mug or plastic tumbler. We carefully stowed one glass with the other crocks in an upper cupboard, but this opened as we drove and, sure enough, when we stopped there it was on the floor in pieces! Next came sleeping bags, pillows, towels, plastic macs, thick sweaters, T-shirts, shorts and bathers. Equally essential were an inflatable boat with paddles, buckets, spades, fishing nets, racquets, bats and balls, as well as a selection of favourite indoor toys. Finally we took considerable quantities of food with us for emergencies, with tins and anything else heavy packed over the wheels to prevent the dreaded 'snaking'.

At length departure day arrived and as we left Swansea and drove towards the motorway, we waited for the inevitable question from the back – 'Are we nearly there?' – and the simultaneous answers from the realistic Gareth – 'We've only just started.' and from me – 'We've done well so far!' We stopped first at the Severn Bridge services, only a couple of hours from home. There we bought lovely chips in cone-shaped containers without bothering to go to the restaurant. Eating these with fizzy drinks, before Bethan and Matthew rolled down a gentle grassy slope, was already a firm holiday tradition. We needed just one more break before reaching the ferry – early as ever.

Boarding was usually an interesting experience, since the crew in their determination to use every inch of space, would beckon Gareth on beyond what he considered to be a safe distance between himself and another vehicle. This year, to his absolute fury, one corner of the caravan roof actually touched the ceiling as he was forced forward. Once parked we hastily grabbed our duffle bags filled with everything we might need on the voyage – returning to the cars during the voyage was forbidden – and joined the mad rush for the best seats on the upper decks. I was left guarding our possessions spread thinly on these whilst the others waved farewell to Britain. Once fairly at sea Gareth rested, but Bethan, Matthew and I explored the ship, clambering rather uncertainly up and down the stairs between decks, and above all seeking the location of a machine which, for a franc, dispensed round, pink sweets quite unknown in Wales. Then we played cards until Matthew's pallor sent us out on deck for fresh air. It was just getting light when we docked, with much repetition of 'Bonjour la France' – and exclamations over driving on the 'wrong' side of the road as we thankfully left the port.

It took us two days, travelling not much faster than 55mph because of towing the van, to reach the Mont Blanc tunnel. Gareth drove solidly each day until late afternoon when we looked in the Caravan Club handbook for the nearest site. Again it was Gareth who, having parked the van – usually with some difficulty! – connected the gas, filled the water container and positioned the waste bucket. I cooked a meal from our supplies and then we were free to enjoy the amenities provided. There were always swings and slides, and usually a pool or stream. Bethan and Matthew were glad to run about, but were in fact never any bother in the long hours spent in the car. For one thing we had a whole range of word games which became more sophisticated as they grew older. However, the main source of amusement was playing the recorder. Both children had been able to play a recognisable simple melody on the kazoo before they could walk and had learnt a basic range of notes on the descant recorder at three. Now, at six and nine – Matthew on violin and Bethan on clarinet – they were in various junior orchestras, thus learning a wide range of music which they could adapt for two recorders. We travelled not only with descant recorders, but treble and sopranino too. Often they played together, sometimes in turns, and I would be honoured with the task of time-keeping – and woe betide me if one had ten seconds longer than the other! Our journeys were enhanced to a great extent by all this music and we listened abstractedly for hours until Gareth, as the driving conditions or his own energy deteriorated, would suddenly say 'I can't stand any more!'

We emerged from the tunnel into Italy at last and selected what was a municipal – rather than Caravan Club recommended – site quite near the centre of Verona. It was excellent and sported a large pool. In record time we were established in our plot and, following instructions, had bought and donned thin, excruciatingly painful, rubber bathing caps. The water was pleasantly warm and emerging into the sunshine after swimming was a true delight. (We have a cine film of this and with what mixed emotions we see Gareth swimming with the rest of us.) Bethan and Matthew were keenly interested in the change of language. Having already visited France a few times, they knew some words and phrases – and from the beginning there had been intense competition about who would wake first and slip out, francs in hand, to the camp shop for 'deux baguettes, s'il vous plaît'. (It was difficult for me to promote fairness while asleep!) They thought it poor of us to have no Italian, but usually managed to communicate with other children in a universal sign language.

The next morning Gareth drove us into the centre of Verona and we took a perfunctory look at what purported to be the very balcony under which Romeo propositioned Juliet! No-one was very impressed and we soon moved on to the magnificent amphitheatre in which there was to be a performance of 'Rigoletto' that evening. Quite without hope Gareth asked if there were any tickets remaining and to our amazement and delight there were! After a restful few hours at the poolside we returned and made our way up and up to the big stone blocks that were our seats. Luckily we had brought cushions from the van or it would have been extremely uncomfortable. We were surrounded by casually dressed Italians, most of whom were enjoying substantial picnics and behaving in a totally uninhibited manner. Gareth and I thought that this cheerful crowd, which could hardly be more different from the staid and formal British opera audience, would prevent us from hearing the distant music – but hardly minded, since it was all such fun. A couple of the nearer Italians presented the 'bambini' with small birthday-cake-type candles. Bethan and Matthew accepted these in a polite but puzzled manner. Suddenly an instant and profound hush fell, the lights went out, and through the darkness hundreds and hundreds of candles twinkled all round the arena, our children's magically lit amongst the rest. From this profoundly moving silence the first notes rose exquisitely, whilst simultaneously, the candles were extinguished and the stage lights raised. Completely in ignorance, as we were, of this opening ritual, it made an unforgettable impact on us all.

Our neighbours, frozen to attention, relished the beauty of the music and applauded with sincere, very enthusiastic warmth. It was heart-warming to be part of an experience of supreme cultural value that wasn't élitist and beyond the means of ordinary people. It's true that the rich and famous exuded glamour in the front rows, but the music was available for everyone. Towards the end, well past his bedtime, Matthew dozed a little. Bethan, three years older, could follow the plot although it was sung in Italian. So, as we stumbled out to find the car, parked quite far away through a maze of streets, I was busy inventing an alternative – this time happy – ending. The person in the sack didn't really die . . . Bethan was just about sufficiently convinced to dry her tears. She knew from the extraordinarily emotive singing of Rigoletto over his daughter that it was a tragedy, but wanted to be comforted.

Gareth always felt that to make full use of a caravan holiday we should stay for several days in three different places of special interest so, after a few more days in Verona, we prepared for the road again and set off to Venice. We camped at Lido di Jesolo in an expensive site where the caravans – mostly highly superior in make – were arranged in rigidly straight lines and few children were about. The atmosphere was unfriendly – so different from every other campsite we've visited – but the weather was superb and we determined to enjoy ourselves in this wonderful location. The next morning we caught a *vaporetto* to St Mark's Square. How we enjoyed the children's delight at seeing the streets really were made of water and their laughter as they stepped on to the landing platform, for all the world as if they were boarding an ordinary bus. It was too hot for us to have much energy for exploring, in spite of sampling what must be contenders for the most costly ice-cream and soft drinks in Europe! We did spend a memorable hour in the Cathedral however, before taking to the water again in a trip up the Grand Canal. We couldn't afford a gondola, but could respond to their romantic image as they drifted past us, and were wholly captivated by the famous bridges and buildings along the sides of the canal. Naturally Bethan and Matthew, well briefed by their father, stared with the fascination of pity and horror at the Bridge of Sighs.

There was so much to see, and after about four days, rather reluctantly, we started our homeward journey – only being glad to leave the prosaic campsite. Gareth was dismayed when the weather changed as we emerged from the tunnel into Austria. For two pins, he would have turned back to the sun, but he had promised that the third part of the holiday would be spent in Salzburg where

Mozart had been born and spent his childhood. The imagination of both children had been caught by this information and indeed they relished the visit to his birthplace, dwelling on, for instance, the kitchen corner where he played as a little child, and his first violin. They begged for a second visit to the house and then wanted a third! It continued to rain and the food in the campsite was expensive, but there was plenty to see. We visited the 'Bishop's Water Palace' at Hellbrunn, where water was used in the most extraordinary number of ingenious ways, from powering complex machinery to dousing unsuspecting guests as they sat at dinner. This was good fun, but our most vivid memory is of Matthew banging his head on a stone balustrade as he raced his sister up a parallel staircase in the palace. His golden hair turned scarlet and we panicked until a passing, kindly, Italian doctor shaved and dressed the area. Suddenly a small voice said 'I don't feel well' and Bethan swayed – we'd been too worried about Matthew to notice her reaction to the accident. I was ashamed of my insensitivity. She had a headache all day, but managed to survive our visit to the salt mines at Hallein that afternoon, without her natural exuberance it's true, but quietly enjoying the cable car, dressing up in white protective clothing, and above all, sliding down into the mines astride a long, substantial, wooden slide which the adults had to use! She did find the guided tour an ordeal though, and unfortunately there was no way to leave the official party once we had started. I wished we had returned to the van. Matthew, of course, showed no ill-effects from his accident.

I could give many, many more details of all we experienced on that holiday, or indeed chosen to describe caravan-based adventures of other years. Yet what I have said should give some idea of what we consider the perfect break. We were in charge, shaping what we did by our own efforts. Though I was the one who, having regularly tasted as a child the freedom of life in static caravans at Goodrington, Lavernock and Saundersfoot, persuaded Gareth to buy a second hand tourer, it was he who put in the physical effort to maintain it. Gareth was, to a huge extent, responsible for how we went and where we went – his historical interests defining the basic route. I found keeping the inside of the van in order and preparing food to be of no trouble, whilst being able to spend long hours playing with the children, almost as a third child, was pure heaven.

These holidays came to an end as the involvement of both Bethan and Matthew in national children's and youth orchestras reduced their free time. Reluctantly, we sold our 'Monza' caravan before it deteriorated, but Gareth and I made a solemn vow to buy another, more luxurious model later on – about now in fact – and start once again. Instead we struggle against almost impossible restrictions and difficulties, as my chapters on a Spanish and a different Italian holiday show. Even if we bought a specially adapted caravan, how could I tow and handle it on my own? Besides, imagine Gareth's frustration at not being able to tinker with the van and car, not even to be able to walk around the site, but sitting – watching and longing. We can't even wander freely through unknown towns without encountering impassable kerbs and inaccessible entrances to most of what we wish to visit. One thing we have lost with a killing finality is our freedom. Our ideal holidays must remain in the past.

5
Conflict and Continuation

The day after Gareth's tracheostomy it was decided to start weaning him off the ventilator. The level indicator of assisted breaths per minute was turned from eight to six, and then to four. We had been warned that this process could be very upsetting to both patient and family, so we doggedly faced up to inevitable suffering, desperate for a successful outcome.

Gareth began the day quite cheerfully. He was glad to be without a collar though the traction hurt his head almost unbearably. A doctor adjusted it about half way through the morning and eased the pain a little. The 'trache' still stopped him speaking but our lip-reading was improving, and by the end of a week I could work out what he said without that too-eager striving for comprehension which makes failure certain. With Gareth in such a desperate state we simply had to know what he was saying, and with only one nurse any good at all at lip-reading, it was up to the family.

The afternoon wore on and Bethan, Matthew and I took it in turns to be with Gareth. We tried to keep his attention away from the reducing number of assisted breaths and reduction of the percentage of oxygen in the air that was being pumped into him. We did not succeed, and by evening he was panicking, gasping for each breath and thinking he wouldn't be able to draw the next one. During those long hours the tension had gradually grown until the three of us, watching in helpless misery, determined to act. Nervously I crept over to the nurse who was busy a little way off: 'Sorry to interrupt, but Gareth can't breathe and he's in a terrible state. Please come to help him.' Instantly she came over, looked at the ventilator, said the oxygen levels were fine and that it was all 'good for him' – part and parcel of a quick weaning off the machine. Before anything more could be said, she was back calmly carrying on with her interrupted task. Matthew was with me at the time and we stared hopelessly at each other. Time passed. Gareth got worse and worse, mouthing that he was dying and imploring me to save him. I felt increasingly frustrated, thinking that surely such a degree of suffering couldn't be allowed even for this highly desirable end. Each breath looked to be his last. At length I caught the eye of Dr Franklin who was walking past. In a split second, merely from my expression, he took in the situation. One look at Gareth confirmed that the process had been too hasty for him and immediately he increased the breaths per minute, oxygen and painkillers, then watched him calm down. He explained they would try again the next day more gradually and that we were not to be unduly worried. Soon we were sent off to bed, with the usual promise of a phone call if we were needed, too emotionally exhausted to think beyond the immediate relief.

Gareth brightened as I entered the ward next morning, but I lip-read that the night had been terrible. A massive dose of painkillers had only a very temporary effect and he had been unable to sleep much of the time. However, he did feel better now and could once more face the reduction of breathing support. Quite soon a rather abrasive and loudly cheerful sister called Mary asked me to accompany her to the small waiting room for 'a little chat'. Wondering what this was about but not unduly apprehensive, I left Bethan and Matthew with their father and followed. She shut the door firmly, asked me to sit down and began, 'The nurses are worried about you. They think you don't look well and are spending too much time in the ward. You can trust them, you know, to care for Gareth and should spend more time out and about.' Taking this at its face value I was rather touched by this concern, but insisted that I was coping adequately. 'I'm infinitely more worried and tense when I'm away from Gareth than when I can see him. I can help too by lip-reading, which I find easy now. And I know for sure he wants me or the children with him always.' I thought the 'chat' was over and that it would certainly not make any difference to the amount of time I spent in IC. With a polite word of thanks I moved towards the door, but seeing her 'cover' had failed she became firmer: 'The truth is that I've had complaints about you. They say you're coming between the nurses and their patient.' I was both astonished and upset, 'How can I? What am I supposed to have done? I only sit quietly talking to Gareth!' 'One of my nurses said you ordered the oxygen to be increased last night. That's interfering with his treatment.' The manifest injustice of this quite took my breath away and I struggled to convince this dour lady that my only positive action had been to catch Dr Franklin's eye and that he, not I, had judged the extent of Gareth's suffering and acted accordingly. I saw that my crime had been to communicate directly with a doctor, rather than through a nurse. Perhaps the latter thought that the resulting action implied a misreading of the patient's condition on her part. I think, in fact, that unable to lip-read, rejecting what I said and relying on machine readings, she had indeed underestimated the extent of his struggle to breathe. However criticism of the nurse had never entered my mind – I just wanted Gareth's suffering to stop.

Mary felt that her job was to protect her nurses and stuck to her point. In effect she was saying that as an interfering nuisance I was no longer welcome in Intensive Care. This was beyond the limits of my endurance and, for the first time, I broke down in front of anyone outside the family. Knowing that there were times in the day when he was not under observation, that he would be undergoing the same awful process as yesterday, that all but one of the nurses couldn't lip-read and he couldn't even call out for help, was more than I could bear. Mary watched my tears and said, 'There's no need to be upset. It'll be the best for all of you.' She quickly disappeared back into IC.

For a few minutes I sat removing traces of tears and wondering how to insist on unlimited daytime access to Gareth. Then I decided the only possible course was to confront the enemy. So waiting until I saw a porter wheeling a trolley into IC, I nipped in after him, walking straight up to Gareth's bed. Almost expecting to be challenged I glanced around, but no one took the slightest notice of me. I had to tell him what had happened and begged him to insist on my right of entry, in the unlikely event of his being able to communicate with Mary.

Bethan and Matthew, as if they had not been sad enough, had this extra burden thrust on them. We had always kept the lowest possible profile, but now, more than ever, resolved to adopt an imbecilic, never-speak-to-anyone (especially doctors), 'fly on the wall' attitude. The three of us also determined that nothing would keep us out of that ward, but profoundly hoped we would not need to battle for it.

The next few days were completely demoralising for us all. They should have been comparatively cheerful since Gareth coped much better with this, the second, reduction of breathing support. But, thanks to Mary, they weren't. The only good thing was that my nervous, close observation told me that she was only sometimes on day-time duty and the same applied to the nurse who had complained. None of us had reduced the number of hours we were with Gareth but the situation was tense. Then one evening a particularly pleasant and sympathetic nurse, Sylvia, glanced sharply at me as she settled Gareth for the night. 'Are you alright? You look terrible.' Normally we would have enjoyed a little harmless chatter as she worked, but since Mary's warning I always tried to remain invisible behind the head of the bed. Without thinking, I blurted out how awful it was to be under threat of eviction from the ward – and not to be with Gareth. She was utterly amazed and said she had never heard a single word of criticism of me – quite the contrary – that the devotion of the whole family was recognised and commended. I was absurdly elated. It looked as if Mary had acted on just the one complaint and everyone else saw me as a willing helper. I can't tell you the difference Sylvia's staunch debunking of any criticism and her gentle confidence-building made to me. That night I went to bed feeling a huge additional load had been lifted from my shoulders – and almost happy.

A day later the 'trache' had been given a 'speaking tube'. If anyone realised Gareth wanted to say something, they could put their finger on the top of this tube, thus diverting the air to the vocal cords. Gareth used his newly-found voice to tell Mary that she was not to upset me. Whether she was sorry for the misery she had caused us all or felt she had made an error of judgement which seemed likely to be taken to higher authorities, I do not know. The situation gradually relaxed and she spoke in quite a friendly manner to me and no more mention was made of interference. She even took time to show me the evidently skilful business of how to wash Gareth ('You take the flannel in your left hand and the soap in the right . . .'!) and once attempted a joke, asking if I was Scottish. Puzzled, I claimed to be Welsh and wondered why she had asked – 'Because you are so sparing with the soap'!

All the time this upset was being resolved, Gareth continued to breathe more easily until on Saturday, 19 July, he managed with no assisted breaths. After the initial attempts the 'speaking tube' would not work, but this didn't matter much because we were now so adept at lip-reading. Gareth had lost all his strength since the accident, to the extent that he could not raise his hand from where it lay, inert, on the sheet. He was pitifully thin and needed as a priority to begin to supplement the drip with food. Even eating was an exhausting activity. Bethan and Matthew would peel and 'de-pip' a single grape from the plentiful supply brought by visitors. For ages he could only eat half of one, in spite of their begging him to try the other half. He simply could not eat. Now at last he began to ask for a little jelly or ice-cream. We could buy the latter in the kiosk on the ground floor and would charge upstairs with it before it melted. Small tubs of jelly had to be bought from town and one or other of the children would go foraging. Later, we moved on to tiny tins of fruit. It was wonderful to spoon a little of this soft food into his mouth and feel he was beginning to get stronger. The canteen sent up food, including chicken soup and rice, fortified by stirring in a nourishing powdered substance. Gareth hated the texture of this thickened food and, if too much powder was added, he couldn't swallow it.

It was clear that he was over the chest infection and, nearly three weeks after the accident, must again turn to the problem of paralysis. This was a dark shadow hanging over each of the four of us in every waking moment. We watched anxiously for any sign of increasing movement or return of feeling. Gareth persisted in the old habit of getting us to touch various areas to test his responses. There was no improvement of any sort and this was more and more depressing as time went on. His main concern was the loss of fine movement in his hands. There was some slight sensation in parts of these but the only approximation to 'true' feeling was in the middle finger of the right hand. The upper side of both hands was completely dead as was everything below the level of the break. One hand was paralysed in a natural-looking, curved position; the fingers of the other were straight and completely rigid. He could not use these hands to do anything at all, which was of desperate significance. What would he do if they remained like this? Our original, all-embracing optimism sometimes, and indeed more than often, moderated to 'If only his hands would move again . . .'

As far as we could see the only positive step towards combating paralysis was the twice-daily provision of visits from members of a team of physiotherapists. Now in the third week of hospitalisation the family were encouraged to watch these sessions. To begin with he was taken through a series of 'passive' movements, arms and legs being manipulated so that if he did regain the ability to move, the muscles would not have atrophied. It was upsetting to see him handled like a puppet – his limbs being bent and stretched, raised and lowered – while he felt nothing. Then, as he got over the infection and began to regain a little strength, the emphasis began to shift towards 'active' movement. Though the physiotherapists continued, for example, to bend his fingers to form a fist, Gareth was asked to struggle with all his remaining strength to slightly move the tip of one finger. Nothing happened. The muscles in the hand were rigid. More hopeful was the attempt to strengthen his arms, because there was some sensation and capability of movement in the upper surface at least. At first it was all he could do to raise a hand very slightly off the bed. Over a few days he began to lift each arm, one at a time. The physiotherapist would hold her hand just above his inert body and say, 'Touch this!' Coordination as well as strength had gone and, for a long time, he simply could not reach it. The family played this 'game' whenever possible and there was great excitement one day when he actually touched two target hands with both of his own. It took weeks to achieve and it seemed hugely important when, much later again, he actually could locate and touch his own forehead. On reflection it also showed all he had lost and the infinite number of difficult, if not impossible, tiny gains needed before he could begin to approach any 'normal' activity. Sometimes it was hard to equate the present feeble invalid with the ever-active person of the past.

Again from the third week we were encouraged to watch the physiotherapists practising their other main function, namely massaging the chest until the phlegm was loosened. This was crucial, because only then was a long, thin tube passed through the 'trache' hole into the lungs, and when it was withdrawn there was a thick, yellowish-grey liquid filling a considerable length of it. The used part was thrown away and the process repeated several times until much less of the tube was filled with each insertion. Occasionally it would scrape the side of the windpipe which would get very sore. I was taught how to suction the lungs in this way in case of emergency, but was not at all confident, fearing to damage a lung – the tube did not slide down the windpipe as smoothly or as readily as I had hoped.

Some physiotherapists and nurses were absolutely wonderful at loosening the 'gunge'. Sylvia, though short and slight, was the champion. She would pummel vigorously at the chest with the edges of her upright hands and bring up yards of noxious fluid, to admiring cries from everyone. How Gareth longed to see her on duty in the evening because it meant a restful night for him. Unfortunately not all the nurses were equally skilful at this and he dreaded the appearance of those who lacked the knack of loosening the phlegm, so failing to suction it into the tube. He knew there would be difficulty in breathing until the next physiotherapist visit, usually not before ten o'clock the next morning.

I think it was 20 July when all the family were watching our favourite physiotherapist, John, at work on Gareth. A tall, dark, young man, he was friendly, sympathetic and exceptionally efficient. Above all he would not stick to his time limit (between twenty minutes and half an hour), but stayed until he was sure Gareth's chest was clear. When things were going badly he would pop in when least expected to perform his life-giving 'miracle'. These extra visits were made in his free time. Once, in all seriousness he said, 'there are some chests I just can't keep away from!' We smiled at this, but felt nearer to tears. There spoke the true professional with deep understanding of the patient's suffering and of the difference he could and would make, even at the cost of hours of unpaid work.

Today he joked cheerily as he performed passive exercises with Gareth's legs. Suddenly, when by chance our three pairs of eyes were focussed on Gareth's right foot, it actually moved of its own accord! The whole family was transfixed with joy, at last scenting an end to our troubles. 'John, did you see that. It moved! It moved by itself! He must be getting better!' John avoided our eyes, 'Well, you see, it's not quite like that. Gareth didn't move that foot. It really did move by itself – without him willing it to happen – or even feeling it. It wasn't a voluntary movement, but a muscular spasm.' He looked sadly round our stricken faces. Then as he massaged the chest he told us hesitatingly that in some patients, and he was careful to stress not all, these muscular spasms grew strong and could become a problem. It was so obvious that he did not want to worry us but felt we should begin to be prepared for what in all probability would be a very difficult future, that I was deeply moved by the rich concern which was the defining mark of his nature. At the same time I despaired that these involuntary movements were incompatible with normal action, rather a regular feature of tetraplegia, and hence another step on the downward path.

A few days later John came to tell us he was being transferred to quite another part of the hospital and wouldn't be able to pop in to give extra treatment to those not deemed to be his patients. Gareth was devastated and tried to give adequate thanks for all that had been done. I only hope John was, and is, fully aware of how much he meant to us all.

During this third week the whole family had become habituated to the tense, nerve-wracking atmosphere of IC. Nothing could have been further from the environment I would wish for sensitive young people. It was impossible for them, as anyone else, to spend so many hours in such a ward without getting emotionally involved with other patients and their relatives. Obviously each bed was occupied by someone who was desperately ill. The policy of the nurses and doctors was, 'Where there's life, there's hope' and they worked feverishly on what seemed utterly incurable cases. I think it true to say, though I may be wrong, that very many of the intake died.

On 22 July all three of us were sitting idly in the waiting room ready to be re-admitted to IC. As usual we had been excluded while a new patient was brought in and attached to vital machinery. We had just about finished a hastily procured drink when two deeply distressed ladies were ushered in by a nurse. She left them after a few kind words and I hesitated over whether we should leave too. The younger of the two was saying, 'Mam, he's in the safest place now. He'll be OK. You've got to stop this crying – it won't help Dad if you make yourself ill, will it?' Slowly the older lady calmed down, and perhaps to give her feelings some relief, was soon telling us the full story. Her husband had seemed to be getting over a major heart attack and had been allowed to leave hospital. Early today he had lost consciousness and was rushed here by ambulance. Already they had been told that several of his organs were in a state of collapse and to expect the worst. No wonder they were upset! What could we say for comfort, except refer to the dedication of the staff, especially Dr Franklin? Over the next three or four days he hovered between life and death. The ladies moved into 'Arosfa' to save a long daily journey 'down the valley'. Regularly we shared the agonies of this family, hearing such details as made us regretfully think that it might be kinder all round to let him die in peace. But we were proved wrong and the ward policy completely justified when the man, before Gareth left IC, had sufficiently recovered to be transferred to his local hospital.

Not so very long after, I came into the ward one morning to see a young man I had not seen before occupying a corner bed. Only his head was visible and it was heavily bandaged. He lay absolutely still and what were probably grieving parents sat at his side. Somehow the atmosphere was particularly grim and Sylvia, who happened to be on duty, whispered, 'That boy was joy-riding on a stolen motorbike last night. There was a gang of them speeding at random round the city. He crashed and got brain damaged. There's no hope. His brain is swelling and nothing in the world will stop it.' She was near to tears, stunned by this pointless tragedy. And he did die some hours later. There was no noise, he just stopped breathing. Again we were asked to wait outside and were amazed to see that the corridor and stairs leading to the ward were lined on both sides with many leather-clad youths consoling themselves with beer or stronger drinks. It was a strange experience, threading our way between these ranks, and they caused some alarm to the hospital staff, but they were silent and stricken with grief. (They did, however, fill the chairs in the waiting room while elderly visitors stood, and left a mess of cans, bottles and crisp packets behind.) They were allowed, a few at a time, into the ward to bid farewell to their friend and I have never seen a more genuine sense of loss. We were struck with the tragic waste of this young life, but almost equally saddened to be told by one pleasantly spoken and sad friend of the dead man that they would be joy-riding again that night.

Without doubt it was the young patients whose plight saddened everyone the most. Only days later another victim of a traffic accident was carried in. He was a good-looking, muscular young man who had been driving his younger sister to school to help his parents. The girl was taken to a local hospital, but he, being more seriously injured, was rushed to CRI. At first he seemed to be paralysed, but to everyone's joy, he began to move his limbs, first slowly and then with vigour. Indeed it became a problem to keep him in bed as he struggled with all his might to get out. The nurses laughed as they wrestled with him, but it was a serious matter stopping him damaging his 'lines'. Soon we wondered why the parents' happiness quickly evaporated – then a nurse told us his injury was to the head and it looked as if he was brain-damaged. Investigations were going on to find the extent of this, but as in Gareth's case, nothing could be finally established until the swelling went down. At least he would live. I spoke at length several times daily with the worried parents and soon I felt close to them as we huddled together in the Maskrey waiting room. They proudly described their son as being in the peak of physical condition, a hard worker and seemingly possessed of every virtue. 'Why should it happen to someone like him?' they kept on asking. Like us, they found it difficult to come to terms with unmerited disaster. Before he was transferred to another hospital he seemed to recognise his parents and say his name, but that was all. We never found out if he got better, though his father had promised to let us know. Assuming his son recovered, and as a way of thanking the hospital staff, he planned to visit the hospital regularly, helping in any way he could. However Gareth was moved to another ward eventually, so we may have missed him if he did come. But I have an awful feeling that the boy stayed brain damaged.

For almost three weeks Gareth was in IC. Whatever his specific condition, death was never far away in that ward. Once or twice we saw the emergency procedure for cardiac arrest. Sometimes we were aware of unusually hectic activity around a patient's bed. At least three times after noticing this we were speedily sent to the waiting room and the door firmly shut. This only happened after someone had died and we would listen for the sounds of the covered bed being wheeled away. Then occasionally the relatives of the deceased would come in and we offered what comfort we could. Usually one of the three main doctors from IC would also come to talk about what had happened and offer sympathy. Sometimes, familiar people would just vanish from the waiting room and we could only assume that the worst had happened for them. The atmosphere was depressing and exhausting, yet most of the relatives and friends were able to sympathise with each other.

If it was terrible for the visitors, what of the staff? Gradually we were getting to know some quite well and learnt how they felt about their demanding work. It seemed that the IC nurses, though seemingly coping with everything, even cardiac arrests, in a matter of fact, positive way could find their jobs very depressing, especially if a series of patients designated to their particular care died. Sometimes they felt as if they were achieving nothing. Once the more fortunate patients began to mend they were moved to other wards or hospitals, so the nurses seldom saw a healthy product of their efforts. On one occasion I thought a particularly friendly and committed nurse was looking decidedly unwell. She explained how she had spent the whole of the previous day sponging blood as it welled out of her patient. I remembered him; his wife had told me all about the massive operation he had seemed to survive so well. But early the following morning he had started to bleed and, though the specialists struggled for hours, it could not be stopped. That night the nurse had vivid nightmares in which she continued to wipe the blood from the dying man. When she got into work his bed was empty. You had to be hardened to survive she said, but sometimes 'it got to you'.

It is quite obvious that Bethan and Matthew had lived through some terrible experiences, not only to do with Gareth. They took it in turns to be in the ward and there was no hiding from them the awful things that were happening all around. Once we insisted they had lunch in town and, in general, tried to encourage them to continue with their own activities where possible. Now we had to insist that Matthew did not miss his National Youth Orchestra course. From the time Bethan was thirteen, one or other, and sometimes both, had played in this orchestra. It was a tremendous honour to be chosen out of young musicians throughout Great Britain. There were three courses a year, one in each of the main school holidays, but in the summer the final concert was a 'Prom' in the Royal Albert Hall in London and this was always the most thrilling experience. Bethan had just reached the retirement age and so, sadly, could no longer play, but Matthew had been looking forward to this NYO course and the National Chamber Orchestra tour which followed. Gareth was absolutely determined he was not going to miss out on these unique opportunities and, at last, won the day. My problem was how to sort out clothes for Matthew, because he had been in Villiers Park for a week and another ten days in hospital where we could only wash underclothes and drape them round our room to dry. Bethan again offered to look after her father and we decided to go on Wednesday the 27th, in the afternoon and return early the next morning. I could wash, dry and iron clothes for the three of us in that time.

I was loth to leave her, remembering the two awful occasions when Gareth was so ill. At least this time he was in IC and Bethan would not stay in the ward at night. Besides, his condition was stable now, as the consultant assured us. Anyway we went and got all the packing done in record time. It was heart warming to see that neighbours two doors away had cut the lawn and hedge, even weeded the path. We caught an early train back. As we waited for entry into the ward, a nurse informed us that Gareth had been moved back to Thomas Andrew ward half an hour previously! An accident victim in a desperate condition needed a bed and, since he was the fittest of the patients at the time, he was chosen to move.

How happy I was that Bethan had not suffered agonies over this change. She knew her father was so much better, at least in respect of his breathing and also that he had gained a little strength. It was wonderful for the three of us to realise that his condition was not considered dangerous any more – so that the move seemed almost to be a 'good thing'. It was also a relief to move freely in and out of the ward without waiting to slip in unobtrusively. But as time elapsed we began to get more and more subdued. He was now in a ward which contained, I believe, more than twenty patients. On duty at any one time were a sister, an auxiliary and a student. How on earth could Gareth get the close observation he needed? He was unable to speak to attract attention and his arm movements were feeble. Suppose he urgently needed help? Eventually we hit upon a solution: if he could push off the oxygen monitor that was clipped to his finger, the alarm would sound and the nurses would come.

Bethan left to stay the night with friends in Bristol, so Matthew and I sat trying to keep Gareth entertained with one eye on the screen which displayed the level of oxygen getting through to his blood-stream. A few times this began to drop, but deeper breathing for a little while cleared the tubes and the level rose again. Two good 'physio' sessions helped tremendously. Quite late in the evening Gareth started to struggle to draw breath and the pulse-oxymeter reading plummeted. I encouraged him to take several deep breaths, but this time the levels continued to drop. Then I made a worrying discovery, namely that the alarm was not working. It should have sounded long before. Because we had been watching the levels so carefully, there had been no time for the alarm to be activated before he had taken evasive action – otherwise we would have spotted this problem earlier. I called the sister who tried to reassure us, saying that she would watch the machine all night. I knew this to be impossible, especially since Gareth's bed was nowhere near the cubicle where the nurses sat. The oxygen intake was already dangerously low and who knew when emergency action would be needed? My heart sank – I would have to impose my will, this time in earnest, once again. Feeling very shaky and mindful of my 'lecture' in Intensive Care, I was exquisitely polite but absolutely determined: 'If it's alright with you, to set my mind at rest I would like to stay all night in the ward with Gareth. Bethan and I always took it in turns throughout the night when he was in Thomas Andrew ward previously. Matthew is here to share the watch with me now, so we'll be fine. We've had lots of sleep recently. We can keep an eye on the level for you.' The whole thing was upsetting, but what else could I do? If the alarm didn't sound, Gareth could deteriorate rapidly. The nurse looked bemused: 'Honestly, I personally will watch him all the time. You need a rest.' I insisted, 'Really, it's no problem for us. We'll stay.' The discussion continued, until recognising my determination, the sister rather resentfully got someone from IC to set the machine properly – it was in perfect working order. I was grateful and extraordinarily relieved. As it was very late by now, Matthew and I reluctantly agreed to rest for a couple of hours. However, I was by no means convinced that Gareth would have adequate supervision in that crowded ward and slept badly. At least with this example of my 'interference' there seemed to be no residual ill-will.

As it happened Gareth survived the night reasonably well, with the machine not alarming very often and, in the daylight, we forgot the worries of the previous evening. Then there was a pleasant surprise in the afternoon; Gareth was given a different kind of 'trache', again with a speaking tube which, hopefully, would be more successful than the last. Gareth was thrilled to have his voice back and become one tiny degree nearer his usual talkative self. Unfortunately his oxygen mask did not work very well, since the elastic which was supposed to clamp it tightly round his face had to stretch round the traction apparatus as well and left gaps. Insufficient oxygen was reaching his lungs and, in any case, the pressure made him panic. Then, a day or two later, this mask was replaced by a nose-tube and, though it delivered less oxygen, it was more comfortable. A suitable collar was found to replace the traction, but this rubbed Gareth's skin mercilessly and we stuffed its edges with cotton wool, so he had a crazy, Father Christmas look.

In spite of all these problems the days passed more cheerfully than might be expected. Gareth was able to chat to his usual procession of visitors; indeed he would become animated and responsive. It is true that his appetite was slight and varied, also his temperature tended to rise and there was a constant battle to keep the chest clear. The medical highlights of each day were the visits of the 'physios', especially the last one, which determined the quality of his night. Everyone feared another chest infection but, temporarily at least, he seemed to be fighting them off.

Never forgotten was the terrible suspense about whether the paralysis would remain. Each passing day of no improvement in movement or feeling meant a slight increase in the probability of this state continuing permanently. Gareth pestered the experts for information and especially for predictions, which were not forthcoming. Visitors brought encouraging stories which gave momentary hope. This big, all-consuming terror was underlying all the other lesser, yet important, hopes and fears concerning his condition. At least for the most part we no longer thought he was going to die. Unfortunately this was to change in the all-too-near future.

Interlude

Journey to Aberystwyth (1992)

Towards midnight a car, with poor visibility, crawled through dense mist and steady, wetting drizzle to the parking space nearest to the door of a block of flats. A fairly smartly dressed woman hastily lifted out, then assembled, a 'push-along' wheelchair, next positioning it very precisely in the small space between the passenger door and the front seat. Reaching for a sliding board, she pushed it gently but firmly under the disabled man and tried to ease him across to the chair. A dead weight, he slumped against the gear lever and, in spite of increasingly feverish attempts, could not be moved. There was no one about, the flats were in total darkness, the damp air invaded the fragile lungs and the rain drifted relentlessly into the car . . .

I woke with a strange air of unreality. Then in a flash I remembered that I was sleeping downstairs in a single bed and that Gareth was at home with me, only two yards away. He had been in hospital for well over five months and yesterday had been discharged. As if this were not sufficiently momentous, we were about to embark on a foolhardy expedition to Aberystwyth. Today was the centenary of the University's Education Department, and there was to be a celebratory dinner including the presentation of a volume of the newly-published history of the department (called *Fit to Educate*) to Gareth. He had told the organiser there was an outside possibility that he would get there, but not to expect him. It was sad to see his state of mind, which compounded a deep longing to be there with a rational assessment of the dangers of such an expedition. I was fully committed to making the journey, thinking it would be a tremendous psychological boost for him to be among his colleagues once more, thus preserving a hope that one day he could take up his professional role again. I also had the strongest possible support for this plan from our friends Margaret and James who were at the scene of the accident, and together we had persuaded the dubious Gareth at least to make an effort to be present.

It had already been arranged that a district nurse would come every morning to get Gareth up. Before she arrived this morning, to my horror, I noticed that there was no urine in the night bag. We realised that the catheter must be blocked. This was an emergency, since the urine would build up in the bladder and cause serious problems. In some ways an in-dwelling catheter was easy to manage, because normally it didn't need to be changed so it was just a case of keeping an eye on the unobtrusive leg-bag and emptying it when necessary. However once in hospital it had somehow got pulled out accidentally, with considerable bleeding, and replacing it, we learnt, was something that required special training which, obviously, I didn't have. Tetraplegics are prone to bladder infections and, I think, some kind of deposit or lining is formed which peels away and blocks the tubes. This had happened several times and, apart from antibiotics, special bladder washes are used which, however, caused different problems later. When, on this particular morning, we told the nurse what had happened, she said that only one nurse in our district could do the job and she wasn't on duty. This was a sad blow to our hopes for the day, but also, more significantly, a very real and immediate danger for Gareth. There was much phoning between different nurses and eventually the only one who could help was tracked down, helping in some charitable concern. To her infinite credit, and our infinite relief, she rushed over in her smart attire to sort out the problem.

As the original district nurse carried on washing and dressing Gareth, I reflected that the same thing would be unlikely to recur in the near future and pressed on with the packing. I did know that there were other difficulties, however. At this stage Gareth's blood pressure was still unstable so that at any moment he could begin to feel light-headed and his vision break up. (He couldn't be left on his own, even for short periods, and until a friend lent me a baby alarm, a five-minute bath was a tense experience and as likely as not I would run up and down stairs a few times, dripping!) I knew well enough by now how to cope with these pressure drops by tipping the wheelchair back until it was almost horizontal and holding it there until he recovered. He was also allowed a limited number of ephedrine tablets which would raise the pressure after about twenty minutes of discomfort. The question was whether he could sit upright through a longish ceremony and the dinner, especially since any food caused his blood pressure to plummet. I was a little more confident about the journey, however, having already discovered that it was possible to tilt the front seat of the car sufficiently far back to effect a recovery. If he did actually faint, which he had never done yet, I wouldn't know what to do, a thought which I must admit was somewhat unnerving.

Gareth's chest at this time seemed to be free from infection and he hadn't needed phlegm to be suctioned through the 'trache' hole for several weeks. Indeed this hole was supposed to be closing up naturally, but was very slow to do so – and it had to be cleaned and dressed daily. If the lungs did suddenly become congested, we would have to seek medical help immediately. We had no idea of the telephone number of a doctor in Aberystwyth and had made no contingency plans in the case of disaster, apart from thinking we would rouse a kind neighbour and ask him to get help. This showed an astonishing lack of forethought on our part, rather than confidence that all would be well.

One final problem was of quite a different sort: namely, driving past the place of the accident. Surprisingly, Gareth had got used to being driven in a car (and by me!) without too much trauma, but actually to re-live the moment of seeing that other car skidding towards him at speed must be deeply upsetting. We discussed other routes, but since this was the quickest he decided to confront the challenge now. On later journeys, as we passed the spot, we have both unintentionally referred to it as 'where we died' – interesting for the 'we' as well as 'died' – and not as histrionic as it seems at first.

Gone were the days of travelling light or easily. It had become and remains a planned exercise. I had packed a huge quantity of medical equipment, including a Spenco mattress, and very few clothes. We had made a check-list of the most important things, but it's always a worry that something essential will be left out. An alarm clock, for example, without which I wouldn't wake to turn Gareth regularly, has enormous significance. However, loading the car was nothing compared with the struggle to get Gareth in it – always a dangerous procedure. The Honda was ruined beyond repair, so our only means of transport was 'my' Metro, which was barely adequate for this purely manual transfer. I had been taught how to do it in Rookwood and found it terrifying. For one thing, there was no way of being absolutely sure the sliding board was secure. If he fell, even on to the rim of the doorway, he could do damage to his skin which would take months to heal. Gareth had no sense of balance and no way of gripping with his hands. His feet had to be lifted in at the appropriate time whilst holding him steady. Another problem was that he was too tall to be held upright as he slid through the doorway. In theory all this should have involved me in little strain, but I tended to try to take his whole weight in case the board moved (in fact, probably making it less secure.) Once he was actually on the seat, I man-handled him into a fairly comfortable position and we were ready.

We would probably never have attempted this trip on our own, but Margaret and James had offered to drive behind us all the way to be with us in the event of an emergency. Parts of the route are comparatively remote and I couldn't leave Gareth in order to get help. They arrived exactly to time and the convoy set off. The journey passed surprisingly quickly and uneventfully, apart from one stop to check the leg bag, which gave our friends a fright since they thought something must be wrong. When we reached the point at which the accident had taken place, Gareth pointed out the exact spot where the other car had suddenly appeared, sliding sideways towards him. In spite of lack of police confirmation we both thought it must have been going too fast to get so out of control. The worst aspect of it all was that it brought out how very unlucky Gareth was to be hit – a few seconds later or earlier, a few yards either way, and he would have been safe. However, perhaps the most important thing was to have driven past the place before a huge psychological barrier could be built about it. Luckily the present was sufficiently demanding to occupy our thoughts, and soon the overwhelming sadness was replaced by eager anticipation and accompanying tension about our arrival at the flat.

After parking in the communal area outside the building, I assembled the chair and managed, by the reverse process to loading, to get Gareth out of the car. We got through the front door – after the usual struggle with a temperamental key and a couple of inner doors – then were relieved to find the lift was big enough for the chair and a standing person. (It would have meant a hasty return to Swansea otherwise.) Luckily too, Gareth could get into all the rooms in the flat, though the narrowness of the corridor made for a small turning circle and I had to lift the back of the chair round many times. It took me several journeys to unload the car. Each time I had to be very careful to take the key because Gareth wouldn't be able to let me in and would be trapped. There would, we assumed, be a spare set of keys somewhere in the building but we didn't know where. With a great sense of relief we enjoyed a quick snack as we worked out the timing for the rest of the day.

Gareth felt he should have a good rest in the afternoon for the skin to be fresh for what might be a long evening. The bedroom, always rather small, had suddenly become microscopic as we positioned the chair next to one of the beds and used the sliding board to get him in. There was little room for manoeuvring but we managed. I checked pressure areas of the skin and found no damage had been done on the journey. Fearing I might sleep through everything, I set the alarm and settled in the other bed. As it happened I was far too 'strung up' to sleep but lay contented, thinking of what we had already achieved.

Later I dressed Gareth into rather more formal attire than he'd worn since the accident. It was tricky getting the jacket on and, indeed, this was the last time it was worn. (Since then we've bought two jackets specially designed for wheelchair users, with short waists and loose-fitting sleeves – at extortionate prices, like everything else made for this comparatively small and not very powerful group of people. The material in these was poor and they were uncomfortable. Gareth refuses to wear them: 'If people don't want me in a sweater, tough luck!') The collar and tie just fitted over the 'trache' hole and he looked smart. I donned an all-too-hastily purchased dress – black with horrible red, yellow and orange flower-shaped blotches – tights and high heels. This was quite unsuitable for what I would be doing. (I have since learnt to dress for comfort and practicality – the popularity of the trouser suit being a great boon for me!) There wasn't much to pack this time, but quite enough: ephedrine tablets, tray, cup, spoon in its wrist strap, urine bottle, sliding board and waterproofs. We struggled along the corridors, down in the lift and into the car. It was a five-minute journey to Old College and, doubtless, the last time Gareth made it, he would have walked.

As I performed the awkward operation of getting Gareth out of the car, porters brought a large ramp for him to get down the quite deep, single step into the building and colleagues appeared from nowhere, offering help which couldn't be accepted. When at length he was established inside and I was surreptitiously trying to tidy his hair (is it better to remain with hair on end and tie askew or suffer the indignity of having it put right for you in public?) many female members of staff embraced him tearfully. The department had in general been very happy under Gareth's direction and he'd shared a mutual respect and affection with his staff. It had been a tremendous personal and professional blow to many when he was struck down. To see him so changed was very upsetting. On the other hand, at times it had seemed that he could die or never get about at all, so there was cause for rejoicing too. This mixture of conflicting emotions was, for me, the continuing distinguishing feature of the evening.

The programme began with a reception at a quarter to six. Then two speakers launched the centenary publication, to be followed by two more speakers who celebrated the tenth anniversary of the Centre for Educational Studies. Between these pairs of speeches the book was presented to Gareth. This was, for everyone (I think) the highlight of the evening. He had, without mentioning it, thought of what he might say. Luckily he had always been able to speak at some length without notes, so that wasn't a problem. But he still had a hole in his throat where the 'trache' had been and air would whistle through this, making it difficult to speak. Also he was breathless at the best of times, so spoke quietly and usually paused at least once in the middle of a sentence. Gareth received the book between the palms of his hands, I gently removed it, and he started to speak almost as before! Characteristically he began with a joke, 'Some people will do anything to park on a double yellow line in Aberystwyth!' Everyone became even more emotional, but he made as beautifully crafted a speech as ever and found breath to deliver it audibly.

The first four speakers had intended to be brief, but there is no such thing as a five minute-speech, especially in Aberystwyth, so the programme was running late well before the actual centenary lecture which was supposed to last three-quarters of an hour. Gareth stayed where he was rather than move to the back of the Old Hall where it was to be held. He was able to chat during this to a much-loved member of the department who was desperately ill. This was the last time he saw her and is another reason why the memory of the evening is so cherished.

It was getting late by the time we came to the meal and musical entertainment. Gareth, who not so long ago had to be persuaded to eat half a peeled and seeded grape, was able to make some inroads into each course and enjoy them. He also had a glass of wine for the first time since the accident. The euphoria carried him along and I had real difficulty in persuading him to leave. He'd been up hours longer than our pressure sore routine allowed and, one day out of hospital, we didn't know if he could get away with the occasional longer time up. Sometimes I suggested he ought to get back to the flat, receiving answers like 'soon' or 'I'm enjoying myself'. It was so wonderful to see him happy with his colleagues again and quite impossible for me to insist on leaving – it had to be Gareth's decision.

At last, well after eleven, we went out into the dark, dank night. I brought the car to the most sheltered position under an archway next to the main entrance and we managed quite successfully to get Gareth and his wheelchair aboard. It couldn't have been more different when we got to the flat. He was wedged securely and, though dreadfully thin at the time, he was too heavy for me to take his weight in that confined space. I was getting thoroughly bedraggled and spoiling my 'tidy' clothes, my feet bare in my ruined tights – not that this mattered in the slightest – but what of Gareth? He was cold and wet, in imminent danger of developing bedsores – and so recently out of carefully controlled, safe surroundings. I had failed in my self-appointed role of giving Gareth some kind of professional life; he would surely be taking a huge step backwards. We were considering whether I should leave him to rouse our neighbours, when, with my last despairing and superhuman effort, he suddenly slid towards me. Thankfully we got through the door and into the hall. Without wasting a second I got Gareth undressed and into bed. His skin didn't seem unduly red, so it looked as if we had got away with our crazy behaviour. Congratulating each other we were soon deeply and contentedly asleep. We had done it!

Luckily we didn't then ask if it were feasible to repeat this kind of strain indefinitely, nor compare it with earlier journeys when Gareth was fit, especially that idyllic day when I was first introduced to Aberystwyth and the future was golden. That happy vision would never return, leaving uncertainty and near despair. Yet already a little had been gained – one day out of a spinal injury hospital and to be making a public speech! It was foolish and could have back-fired, but luckily, it did not. Instead it was a kind of landmark showing everyone that though Gareth was disabled in body, his mind and spirit were still 'alive and kicking'.

6

Bute and Farewell

Monday, the first of August, began cheerfully. Gareth made a big effort to be at his best before Matthew left for NYO. Bethan had been in Swansea the previous evening for her Karate session, slept at home and had ridden her horse, Flicka, that morning before catching a train back to Cardiff. Her early return meant we were all together for a few hours and we talked and laughed in a hopeful frame of mind. In the early afternoon James, on one of his regular visits, kindly took me to the station to see Matthew off. I made the usual promise to telephone regularly and to tell the truth about his father's condition, however unpalatable. When we got back to the hospital, Gareth was being entertained by Bethan's martial arts stories and still seemed reasonably comfortable. At about five o'clock he felt tired and drifted into a shallow sleep. After fifteen minutes he woke with a racing pulse.

All day his temperature had been slightly raised and he had constantly demanded drinks. No one was alarmed by this, however, and Gareth explained his thirst in terms of the nose-clip making his mouth dry. Now Bethan and I felt uneasy and tried to lower the pulse-rate, especially by encouraging him to listen to the Test Match through ear-phones. (Fairly certain, I thought, not to arouse much excitement!) In the past, following cricket was a seldom-to-be indulged treat; now he couldn't concentrate on the game at all. He was only aware of that pulse getting faster and faster – and began to panic. This made the situation even worse and I felt a vicious circle was developing: the fast pulse caused the panic which increased the pulse which deepened the panic . . . When the nurse on duty actually measured the pulse, it had reached a hundred and fifty! She was alarmed and sent for a doctor. He came quite quickly, examined Gareth, gave him an injection and went away leaving the pulse getting ever faster.

Now the curtains were pulled round the bed and a whole series of experts, including a registrar, came, but could not understand what was happening and vanished. Bethan and I were sent to the visitors' room; a long, thin room which always smelt of smoke in spite of the 'no smoking' sign. This was right next to Gareth's bed so we listened intently through the open door and, indeed, crept out to pace around the outside of the curtain, looking through a gap from time to time. A physiotherapist, one of our favourites, came for her usual evening visit and worked on his chest for a while, but this made no difference to his condition and she joined us. Unwilling to leave until he was better, she tried to speak encouragingly, but clearly was very worried indeed. By now the pulse rate was over two hundred and still rising. Gareth gasped piteously. Nobody could do a thing about it.

My greatest frustration was that IC was not a hundred yards away, and I had the utmost confidence that they would diagnose the situation at a glance and have a remedy at hand. None of the other doctors who had tried to help and failed, knew anything about Gareth's medical history except what was immediately visible. Bethan and

I kept pleading with the various doctors, 'Please will you send for Dr Franklin? He'll know what to do.' The answer always was, 'No one is ever allowed to disturb the Intensive Care staff. They've got more than enough problems of their own.' 'But could you just send to ask for advice? He's getting worse and worse. Please!' Nobody would break the rule and it was getting to be more than we could bear. From the beginning it had been terrible to feel and see the unnatural vibration in Gareth's skin, to see his hectic colour and to witness the huge effort needed just to breathe – and the pulse-rate had doubled since then. Gareth lay conscious but terrified whilst he listened to the growing body of experts expressing their bewilderment about what was wrong with him. Bethan and I, outside the curtain, gave up all pretence of being in the visitors' room. Everyone was too worried to send us away. Bethan voiced her fear, 'Mum, if that pulse gets any higher, he'll die. We can't stand here and let it happen. You've got to get Dr Franklin whatever they say!' We were both at breaking point. She was right, 'O.K. Beths. I'll get someone from IC.'

Resolutely I walked towards Intensive Care. Despite my absolute decision to the contrary, I was going to 'interfere' again – and I would bring someone to Thomas Andrew ward who could save Gareth whatever it took. I had no plan and I was delivered from having to take IC by storm for, by the greatest stroke of luck, I met one of its experts in the corridor. She, Gwenda, was an anaesthetist who had often attended to Gareth, and we had complete faith in her ability and compassion. Hearing my distraught account of Gareth's state, we hastened together to Thomas Andrew. Quickly she examined Gareth and, luckily, had the power to order that he should be sent back to IC as a matter of urgency.

I was convinced for eight years that my 'accidental' meeting was instrumental in this, but meeting Gwenda at the swimming baths some time ago, she remembered the incident but thought she had been on her way to Gareth before she saw me. Whatever the true explanation, we will always believe that she saved his life and feel a tremendous debt of gratitude to her. Immediate admittance to IC was always difficult because it was invariably full. At length, an elderly lady was sent to an ordinary ward and Gareth wheeled in. It was half-past midnight, seven and a half hours after his symptoms started. Instantly he was plugged into a ventilator and heavily sedated.

Bethan and I had been asked to wait in the familiar Maskrey visitors' room until a nurse could see us. A long, long hour later she told us not to worry, since it was probably a minor hitch. Gareth would once again be weaned from the ventilator as soon as the cause of the racing pulse was identified and sorted out. We appreciated her kind intentions but saw no reason for optimism and crawled into bed feeling totally defeated. My only cheering thought was that Matthew was away from the protracted tension and misery of the day. In his brief phone call to tell us he had arrived safely, I had concentrated on what he was doing and simply said that his father had a bit of a temperature and his pulse rate was up, but doctors were sorting it out. Matthew's time would already be fully occupied, so I could feebly hope that he was not too depressed. The crucial question now was what effect all this was having on Bethan. Having done our best, throughout her childhood, to protect her from the darker experiences of life, we had now unintentionally exposed her to the very worst. Thinking of this along with Gareth's seemingly hopeless state, made those few minutes before the craved oblivion of sleep as bad as any I have lived through.

Early the next morning we were back at our old post outside the door of Intensive Care waiting to creep in surreptitiously. Gareth was still under heavy sedation and didn't respond to us until much later in the day. Test results from the previous day's panic measures began to arrive. It was not until after two that a doctor reached him that day and he told us that the problem had been a severe chest infection which had developed into septicaemia. Though this was dangerous, it was even now under control through a large dose of antibiotics. It was very worrying to hear this because Gareth had only just stopped the medication for the last infection. We feared it would be a permanent problem and the severity of the symptoms would be impossible to handle outside hospital – and almost so inside, for that matter.

To our surprise, Dr Franklin changed the diagnosis the next morning. He said that, though Gareth did have an infection, it was not this which had caused the remarkably high pulse rate. Rather, it was the result of an imbalance of drugs. In the cocktail prescribed in IC, there was one which was responsible for controlling the pulse, and this had inadvertently been discontinued in Thomas Andrew. He apologised for this, saying 'We've let you down.' It would have been easy to let us continue believing the false, but worrying explanation, and Gareth saw it a mark of the integrity and supreme concern of the man that he told us the truth, though it meant admitting his team had made a mistake. We were truly thankful and more optimistic that Gareth would quickly return to his previous condition.

Dr Franklin suggested taking him off the ventilator at one fell swoop and fitted him up with a cigar-shaped oxygen tube. He was able to breathe fairly comfortably using this and spent the next night without any additional support. However, the following few days were daunting. From time to time he had to return to the ventilator and huge quantities of sputum had to be suctioned from his chest. It was not going to be as easy a return to independent breathing as we had hoped. Bethan and I developed a dull, habitual acceptance of Gareth's just-about-living state. We talked and talked together about everything, trying to be positive, but despair often broke through the surface of our composure – it was over a month since the accident and there was no improvement.

For two whole weeks Gareth remained in IC. It was not that his condition warranted such treatment. The desperate shortage of finance in the hospital meant cuts in nursing staff and, to the complete frustration of Dr Franklin and his colleagues, one of their beds had to be 'closed'. He expressed his feelings to us, finding it hard to accept that, with many desperately ill people clamouring for admission, one of his beds, surrounded by vital equipment in perfect working order, lay empty. It was moving to observe the obvious depth of his emotion. Yet the situation worked to Gareth's advantage as he grew stronger. For, instead of being sent back to Thomas Andrew, he was allowed, unofficially, to occupy the 'closed' bed and such nursing as he required was fitted in as extra duties for the rest of the staff. Everyone must have accepted the situation gladly and there were certainly no complaints. In fact he became the established 'pet' of the ward! It was such an unusual pleasure for the nurses to have a patient who could speak, even joke, with them and be aware of, and grateful for, their services. They seemed to gravitate to his bed whenever there was a quiet moment. Sometimes one or another would bring a tempting 'treat' from town or home; sometimes he had a flower on a nicely-arranged breakfast tray.

A week after Gareth was re-admitted to IC, Matthew's NYO course was to end with a Prom. We had never missed a final concert in the Albert Hall ever since Bethan had joined the Orchestra. It was a traditional family occasion, with the long drive from Swansea and the pre-concert meeting in the foyer. The gigantic, circular hall was always packed and the promenaders entertaining to watch until the concert started. The standard of the playing was exceptionally high, not only because all the players were very talented but because they would have rehearsed this programme solidly for about ten full days (a luxury often denied professional orchestral players who sometimes have to perform after a very small number of rehearsals). Perhaps most memorable, however, was the emotional quality and vitality of the performance, largely a product of the youth and undimmed enthusiasm of the players. When it was all over we would join a huge crowd of other parents waiting for their children. The disadvantage of the Albert Hall in this context is that as a circular building it has numerous entrances. We would first converge on the Artists' entrance, but after a while players would emerge from different doorways and in the end there would be a mad rush from door to door. Bethan and Matthew always seemed to be among the last to appear. There would be a prolonged series of embraces and farewells, before the search for the car in the all-too-similar streets radiating out from the building. The excitement would diminish as we drove down the M4 and, by the time we reached a suitably distant service station, we would be too tired to eat.

This year was going to be different. At first we thought none of the family could possibly attend, but after several days in IC, Gareth's general health was so much better that he wanted Bethan and me to support Matthew. He would listen to the radio broadcast from his bed. Again Margaret and James, the friends who helped at the scene of the accident, came to our rescue. They had a flat in London and offered to meet us at Paddington, take us to the Prom, meet us when it ended and drive us to Cardiff on their way back to Swansea. They made light of the enormous inconvenience this involved and we were very glad to accept, since it would cut down the time away from Gareth drastically. Because he was much more stable now, Bethan and I were able to make this decision without too much worry – after all he was in the safest possible place! Everything went according to plan and we found Matthew quite a while before the concert began. This time the previous year Bethan had been principal clarinettist, so she knew most of the players and probably all the staff. The latter had heard about the accident and were very kind to her now, having also kept an eye on Matthew throughout the course. It was a strange experience for Bethan not to take an active part in the occasion she had so deeply relished in the past, but she enjoyed the music: Berg's 'Three pieces for Orchestra', and especially Mahler's 'Symphony No. 2' with its strongly dramatic impact. Matthew appeared at the end with all his possessions, glowing with the after-effects of such emotional playing and the three of us were driven safely back to hospital by about one o'clock. During much of the concert I had thought of Gareth lying motionless, listening avidly and longing to be with the family. I thought further back to the last Prom when he had taken his usual active role in getting us there and back. It had been televised and the video recording not only shows both children playing, but at the end, pans around the audience revealing Gareth and me applauding wildly – a visual testimony to the way things once were.

We knew there was no hope of seeing Gareth that night so, having amazed the security guards, we made straight for our tiny room and found enough space in which to sleep. Matthew was leaving again in the late afternoon of the following day, this time to embark on the National Chamber Orchestra's tour of Switzerland. He wanted to spend as much time as possible with his father, while I did what I could to wash and iron his clothes. (We had discovered a small laundry room and had asked permission to use it.) Gareth and he chatted at length about every detail of the course, the concert and the kind concern of all the staff. When he had to catch his train he was very reluctant to go, but everything had been arranged long before and Gareth was certain Matthew would enjoy the tour once it started. As we kept saying, it did not take more than a couple of hours to get from Switzerland should the need arise. I went with him to the station, then Bethan and I settled once more into our hospital routine.

Gareth's concern that Bethan and Matthew should continue to have some sort of life outside hospital threw his own shrunken existence into stark relief. Since he could only lie absolutely still, with his position changed marginally every few hours, apart from human contact, he had only the radio to while away the long and not too cheerful days. Even this was not much good since the headphones tended to slip off and he had to wait for someone to reposition them for him. Dr Franklin's remarkable care for his patients extended beyond the physical and he kept trying to improve Gareth's 'quality of life'. One day, for instance, he offered to set up a television set high above the bed. In fact Gareth declined, thinking it would be too difficult to keep it in his line of vision as he could not move his head at all to accommodate the shifts in his position. But he did appreciate the kindness of this idea as of all the little 'extras' by which the staff tried to enliven his day.

Gareth's deepest need continued to be having a member of the family at his side. Forgetting the terrible day when I had been banned from the ward, one of us was virtually always with him, from the time we were allowed in until the lights were dimmed for the night. Bethan and I became accepted as features of the ward and sometimes were even quite useful. For instance, we could form part of the chain of four or five nurses who synchronised their movements to change Gareth's position slightly. We were allowed any part of the body but the head in this manoeuvre. Also we would usually feed Gareth, thus saving the nurses time, and we often shared jokes at the food. Once he made a face at some red jelly he was being fed, and in a spirit of fun a nurse tasted it. Salt had been put in instead of sugar! This became a great source of amusement for succeeding shifts. In our early days in IC we would never have envisaged such comradely moments, but so it was.

It was getting towards the time when the traction could be removed since the neck would have fused into its new position. One day there was a loud crash and the weights had fallen to the floor! At first there were moves to reposition them by re-attaching the clamps to Gareth's skull, but then X-rays were taken and a new, hard, supportive collar was fitted instead. It was pure heaven to be released from that permanent pressure on the head and neck, but the collar was very abrasive to the skin and once again we packed it full of cotton wool to ease the problem. What excited us was the thought that without the weights it should be possible for Gareth to sit up. After six weeks of his lying prone this aim assumed gigantic proportions. Surely his quality of life would be infinitely better and surely his chances of recovery must blossom. Once again we were somewhere near happiness, but soon this evaporated as the nurses hit on a snag. The rigid collar had no hole in it for the oxygen tube to pass through. It was an impasse. He needed the collar to be able to sit up and he needed the oxygen in order to breathe. The hospital was ransacked, not for the first time, to find a suitable collar for Gareth but without success. The whole family was locked into the conviction that he would never be upright again and felt utterly depressed. What sort of life was possible if you could only lie flat? It was too awful to visualise.

After a day of misery, Bethan and I entered IC to find a beaming Dr Franklin carefully attaching an intricate system to Gareth's 'trache'. Not one to be bound by conventional techniques, he had creatively managed his resources to solve the problem. Some nurses were watching with obvious admiration. 'You'll probably feel dizzy at first, after lying flat for so long,' he warned a grateful Gareth. Two nurses carefully cranked up the head of the bed just slightly and watched for any worrying reaction. He was indeed very disoriented, but eventually did become acclimatised to this different position. During the day the bed was gradually raised to about sixty degrees from the horizontal. He was elated saying, 'I feel so much more civilised upright! And the ward looks so strange from this perspective – I could hardly see anything before.' But by the evening he was totally exhausted from this 'new' experience. It seemed such a tremendous advance that Bethan and I (and Matthew when we told him by phone) were ecstatic and could hardly praise Dr Franklin sufficiently.

Next day was even more significant. I helped dress Gareth into pyjamas – the first time he had worn anything since his accident (to avoid marks on the skin). Several nurses lifted him out of bed and placed him in the one ward armchair, a reclining Parker-Knoll with a footrest. It was hard to believe – he was actually sitting in a chair! A tube from the catheter was attached to his leg, an enormous collar sprouting clouds of cotton wool hid his neck and lower face, and an oxygen supply was somehow channelled into his lungs, but he was sitting up. The time out of bed was slowly increased and everyone's optimism soared. Going along with this was a steady decrease in the flow of sputum and a general increase in strength and appetite. After a few good days there was talk of Gareth being transferred once again to a ward with less intensive nursing. The 'closed' bed he was occupying was now to be 're-opened', so in all fairness he must give way to a seriously-ill patient. We all felt he would be leaving a safe environment where he had been appreciated and pampered, but were full of gratitude for those two weeks in which we knew experts were doing all that was possible to return him to a condition where the basic problem of paralysis could be tackled. Yet it seemed to us that, in one sense, all the time since the accident had been wasted – he had only got infinitely worse before being brought slowly back to his state immediately after impact.

The ward to which Gareth was taken on Saturday, 15 August, was called Bute. He was wheeled on a trolley into a corner just inside the door and lifted on to a bed while I put his possessions into a locker. I was alone as Bethan had gone to Swansea for her Karate session and would return a little later; Matthew was still in Switzerland. Naturally, after the experiences of the last sortie into a 'normal' ward, Gareth and I were both rather apprehensive and, as it happened, the first sight of the new ward couldn't have been more daunting. As the porter and nurse vanished with the trolley, we stared around in dismay. What appeared to be two long rows of fit, young people each having the odd bandaged limb, seemed to be reclining with parties going on round their beds. It was quite noisy, with much chattering and laughing. Everyone turned to see what the newest patient was like. Gareth was by far the fittest patient in IC and, psychologically, this was very good for him. Now, in this new context, his disabilities became more evident than ever before. He felt, and was, conspicuous in his difference from the others. It was clear to me that he was desperately upset and I was not much better. How on earth could he survive here?

As we struggled to come to terms with this alien environment, a nurse pulled the curtains around the bed, sat down and began to fill in a questionnaire. 'Can you walk?', 'Can you feed yourself?', 'Can you use the lavatory?', 'Can you wash or dress yourself?' The list went on and on but the answer was always 'No.' To the nurse this was an objective gathering of information about his condition, but it was infinitely depressing for Gareth. I felt frustrated at not being able to stop his suffering. At last the questions did come to an end, but before we could draw breath someone else came with a similar list and he had to go through the negative responses again. (I believe there was a third list, but can't be quite sure.) By now Gareth was determined not to stay in Bute and began to demand to be taken to Thomas Andrew or anywhere else where the patients did not appear to be in splendid general health, having one minor injury. The staff, rather patronisingly, said he would get used to it.

We were not immediately impressed with the two nurses we first encountered. One seemed a self-assured, perky, young man who was out to make an impression on everyone. The other was an equally young woman with vividly dyed hair and heavy make-up. I didn't really fancy the idea of either of them nursing Gareth and, emphatically, nor did he. We were both on the verge of tears and devastated by this vivid insight into the life he would have to lead if he did not recover – the lists underlined that he could do none of the ordinary things that normal people perform so unthinkingly day by day.

The final straw came about half an hour after we arrived. The male nurse, seemingly exhilarated by his importance, was showing a group of students around. He stopped at the first (Gareth's) bed and, in a carrying voice, detailed all his disabilities, not addressing him directly at all. As if this was not bad enough, showing off, he said, 'Have you heard of ankylosing spondylitis? It's a condition in which the spine gradually becomes fused. Can you imagine sinking a pint in that condition?' He went through a macabre pantomime, bending at the knees and leaning back with a straight spine while he 'drank'. The students thought he was droll and laughed. I wonder I did not attack him verbally or even physically, but I suppose it was too painful for action. The group moved on. Gareth and I stared at each other and tears welled up in our eyes. He muttered savagely, 'Get someone from Intensive Care. I'm not staying here.' In complete agreement, but with sinking heart at having to assume yet another difficult role, I left.

Luckily, for the second time at crucial points in this saga, I met one of the very best nurses from that ward. She, no doubt on her way home, came with me to Bute. Gareth poured out his emotions until she, too, became tearful. Eventually she said, 'I agree this is the wrong place for you and I'll see that you're moved. But you were only sent here because Thomas Andrew was full and, as it's Saturday, it's very difficult to get anything organised before Monday. Is there any chance you could put up with staying here just for today and tomorrow? It would be a real help all round.' Put like that by someone who knew and cared for him, what could Gareth do? Sadly he agreed to do his best. Luckily we had all calmed down by now and somehow felt we would manage between us.

During the weekend the news that Gareth was unhappy in Bute spread back to IC. Several nurses and doctors kindly came to cheer him up on more or less social visits made in their own time. Oddly enough, however, it was not as bad as that first impression. The female nurse turned out to be kind-hearted, brisk and efficient. Though the male one could hardly develop a sympathetic sensitivity overnight, he worked hard and did his practical best for his patients. For instance he took pride in shaving Gareth closely, joking at the efforts of the female staff (and mine). He even insisted on washing Gareth's hair for the first time since the accident, making channels of plastic sheets and using lots of water which cascaded down from the head of the bed into a bowl. I never forgave him his stupid parody of Gareth's illness, but he had many good points.

We soon got used to the inevitable limitations of being nursed in a crowded ward, though we found once again that the clip fitted to Gareth's finger to monitor the level of oxygen in his blood did not trigger the pulse oxymeter alarm. I was obliged to go through the 'I'll stay up all night' pantomime until it was fixed. Dr Franklin's superb, newly-invented oxygen feed, which had been brought to Bute's storeroom, had been thrown out by another nurse in a fit of tidiness. This would delay Gareth's sitting up until it was replaced next day. Bethan and I were persuaded to leave the ward after eleven to get some sleep and were fairly, but by no means wholly, confident that he would be comfortable through the night.

The next morning, Sunday, Gareth was looking forward

to sitting up as soon as breakfast was over and his oxygen supply fixed. However, we hit an unexpected snag. The only suitable chair was the Parker-Knoll in IC. I offered to get it immediately, as it was a very short distance away and Bethan would help, no doubt finding it a very trifling weight. This was not allowed, nor could two nurses fetch it, because only the porters were insured against injuries sustained in moving furniture. It appeared later on, together with a Ro-ho cushion for Gareth to sit on. He was soon lifted onto this and stayed up for many hours.

By Monday when the offer of a transfer to another ward was made, Gareth was sufficiently used to the place to decide not to cause extra work. Some of his fellow patients came over to chat and others waved from their beds. Most of the fittest were discharged and a handful of more seriously ill people took their places. He no longer felt so conspicuous because of the extent of his disabilities and began to feel more at home in his corner. The atmosphere was lively and varied compared with the subdued hush of IC. One cleaner was a particular source of amusement. She would sing at the top of her voice and make jokes as she worked. With a great air of thoroughness she would pull all the beds and cupboards into the middle of the ward, only to find she had no time to clean the areas thus cleared, and so push them back again!

Another reason why it was not worth changing wards was that Gareth's time in CRI was drawing to a close sooner that we expected. More and more references were being made by nurses, doctors and physiotherapists to rehabilitation and somewhere called Rookwood where this was to take place. Gareth was told it was a tough regime, upholding the 'no pain, no gain' theory. For instance, he would be told to propel his wheelchair to physiotherapy using hands and arms, and would simply have to get there, however hard the struggle, thus exercising the heart and building muscles. We had no means of visualising what this might be like and started to get apprehensive. Dr Franklin came for a farewell chat with Gareth and gave him some final advice: 'Stop being Mr Nice Guy. Change your character, demand, browbeat . . . It's the bastards who survive!' I was a bit worried by this, not quite seeing Gareth in his present state as capable of making aggressive demands. But this farewell, as every other contact with Dr Franklin, deepened our awareness of his brilliance and individuality – and our fervent thanks were quite inadequate to the debt of gratitude.

The nurses, whether on purpose or not, were getting us accustomed to hearing Gareth described as 'disabled'. They would kindly tell us that so much more was being done nowadays for 'people like Gareth'. Underneath such remarks was a horrible undercurrent of acceptance that his condition was permanent. I would inwardly and bitterly rebel against this, saying over and over to myself, 'He is not disabled, he is not disabled. He will get better. There is still a chance.' I particularly hated the concept of 'rehabilitation' with its implication of an irreversible, damaged state, wanting fiercely, though perhaps irrationally, to replace it with 'recovery'.

On 21 August I took taxis and train to Pennard, returning in my Metro. Our friends the porters reserved a place in the tiny car park outside the main entrance of CRI. Bethan and I packed the possessions that had amassed in the seven weeks we had lived there and loaded them into the car with most of Gareth's things, since only one bag would go with him in the ambulance. Just one week after entering Bute, he was transferred to a trolley and wheeled out of the building. So, paralysed, skeletal and just about able to breathe on his own (the 'trache' having been removed by Dr Franklin two days previously), he was driven off by ambulance to Rookwood. The future remained unbearably uncertain, above all in connection with Gareth's health, but also in terms of finance – how and where would we live? Our careful planning had disintegrated in the face of disaster and there seemed to be no sustainable hope, as up to the accident there had always been, that 'things would work out for the best'.

Bethan and I took a final glance at the place where we had suffered for the whole summer and where Matthew had shared much misery. In the early days I had paid a few visits to school and later on attended Bethan's graduation and Matthew's 'Prom'. Matthew had been more or less forced by his father to attend the high-level music courses. Bethan had sometimes ridden her beloved horse and got to some karate sessions in Swansea, also joining a Cardiff leisure centre for more karate and 'keep-fit' sessions. She had even celebrated her twenty-first birthday in a hospital ward, sharing the cake with the nurses! She continued with her plans to study for an MA degree in Bristol. But in spite of these rare excursions into the 'real' world, we had mostly lived in despair, in the confines of CRI. We had all tried to keep up an appearance of bright optimism, but sensed with unerring accuracy the bursts of misery that overtook the others when alone in our room. Most vivid is the memory of one time when our defences crumbled and we agreed in all sombre, loving seriousness that it would be better for Gareth to die than to remain as he was. Matthew missed some of the worst periods, but he, as Bethan, had gone through experiences that would mark the most affectionate natures who had firmly believed in the ultimate benevolence of the world.

Cardiff Royal Infirmary is no longer a hospital. When we were there it was under threat, much to the dismay of everyone – nurses, cleaners, physiotherapists, porters and doctors. Though the building was generally held to be inconvenient and probably expensive to run, there was a tradition of caring that was dear to the people of Cardiff and far beyond. If we are typical of patients and grieving families, there must be an enormous sense of loss at its closure, and gratitude (in our case, with one notable exception) for the treatment and sympathy so generously bestowed.

Interlude

Independence

An academic worked in his room, high up in one of the twin towers of a Victorian university building until nine o'clock. It was dark, as all the corridor lights had been extinguished by this time. The late worker knew the position of the switch for the steep spiral stairs, but not for the main stairs, so he had to feel his way cautiously down and then across the quadrangle on the ground floor. It was rather disturbing being alone in the old, silent spaces, and occasionally a thought of what would happen if he fell edged into his mind. Reaching the big, wooden door at last, he felt for the lock. Eventually he re-locked it securely behind him, and with a sense of relief, walked briskly away through the streets. He enjoyed the freshness of the night sea-side air, the freedom from the hours of concentrated thought – and, having called in for a Chinese takeaway, continued to a lonely, but short evening in his flat. Probably no one would pinpoint the independence of this man as a salient feature of the scene, yet, quite unconsciously, it was assumed to exist.

Gareth's work had, at home, always been considered to be more or less sacrosanct. His wages kept the family going. Without being unpleasantly competitive, he had always worked to win promotion and he had been successful. Gradually he moved from being an assistant teacher in John Ruskin Grammar School in Croydon, through various stages, to a Chair of Education at Aberystwyth University. This was obviously due to his ability and industry, but also partly because he was comparatively free to pursue his career.

Being in an Education department meant that there were two major parts to the job, and clearly, both made large demands on Gareth's time. First there was the business of teaching graduates how to become teachers themselves. In those days, those students would spend considerable time in the department having lectures and tutorials, not only on the most obviously relevant practical questions of method and matter, but also on equally important more theoretical subjects, such as the philosophy, psychology and history of education. When the students were at schools on teaching practice, the tutors would observe them teach and give advice and encouragement. I would sometimes smirk when Gareth admitted to tiredness having 'seen three lessons', thinking he should remember what it was like to teach them! However, these schools were often quite distant from college and each other. Also I did know really that to sit at the back of a lesson, identify its good and bad features, and give positive yet sympathetic advice could be demanding, especially if there were serious problems. Then, of course, a detailed report had to be written for the student and an official copy kept. Finally there was the setting and marking of essays, which could be very time-consuming. There were some fixed points in Gareth's week, like lectures and tutorials, but he had some freedom in, for instance, planning his teaching practice timetable and deciding when to do his preparation, marking and record-keeping.

The other major part to the job was academic research. Until fairly recently the amount of research work expected to be undertaken by lecturers in the education department was not made explicit. Some people put all their energies into the teaching side, but Gareth wasn't of this number. Ever since his initial degree he had been deeply involved with writing books and articles. One reason for this was his quest for promotion, because the number and quality of publications were the main criteria here. However, he would often say how lucky he was that his chief leisure interest and his work were one and the same.

It was, and is, impossible to make any significant research contribution without working long hours outside the time spent in the department undertaking formal commitments. Bethan and Matthew grew up knowing that if Dad was in the house, the chances were that he was doing, what Matthew as a small boy called, 'scribbling in the study'. I would try not to disturb him, frequently creeping in with cups of tea, each one accompanied by a Kit-Kat. If the children needed their father for anything, they would burst in upon him and he wouldn't be annoyed unless at some crucial point in his work – or, for instance, as happened once, he had just lost seven hours of writing on his newly-acquired word processor! Somehow the interruption would be short lived, though, as they knew he should be left in peace. Often he would work late into the night or sometimes spend an evening in his college room where most of his books were kept. Even in vacations he would only take a few weeks break at most. Often he would work with documents in the British Museum or Public Record Office, whilst the rest of us would enjoy ourselves at home or with relations at Walthamstow, Coventry, St Albans or Cwmbran.

In spite of Gareth's wholehearted involvement with his work, he was a family man, part of a very strong unit. Once Bethan was born, we accepted, to what even then was a surprising extent, the traditional division of roles, where Gareth was the wage-earner and I the home-maker. However, the edges of this categorisation were always blurred, since, for instance, I always did some part-time teaching, mainly in the Open University and later in schools. When I was at work, luckily mostly in the evenings, Gareth tried to arrange his commitments so he could be with the children, particularly in their babyhood. In general, however, I was home-based and Gareth got on with his career. As it happened, this suited me very well. Apart from my own idyllic childhood, I had never been so content. From about mid-morning, when I had finished my hasty attack on whatever housework was absolutely necessary, we were free. Most fine days were spent on our local, perfect beaches. In the summer, we splashed about in the sea, made castles in the sand and explored rock pools. When the weather was cold but dry, we adventured along the cliffs, built wood fires on the pebbles and ate lovely, smokey, blackened food. If we were stuck indoors, we spent long hours at our dining table, engrossed in messy, creative activities. I could do all my favourite things and, at the same time, think I was providing Bethan and Matthew with enriching experiences!

Because I was by nature happy at home, Gareth was free for the most part to organise his time without much attention to the minutiae of the home scene. Yet there were things he did contribute and, obviously, these varied over the years. For instance, when Matthew was born, it was quite difficult at times to cope with a baby and a toddler just turned three. We still, for Bethan's sake, often went to Three Cliffs or Pobbles beaches, but it was one thing to get the pushchair down the fairly steep slope, with Bethan running around happily, quite another to drag it up in the late afternoon with two tired children and mountains of equipment. If Gareth could occasionally join us for an hour and help on the trek home, it made such a difference. Once Matthew could walk a reasonable distance, we could manage most expeditions without help, so Gareth could decide for himself whether he could allow himself the luxury of an extra hour or so away from his work. I soon learnt there was much more happiness all round if his frequent decision that he couldn't spare the time for some pleasure trip or another, went unchallenged. We would meet up later in the day, all equally satisfied – and I certainly felt myself to be the luckier of the two. As time went by and the children developed their own interests, we were both frequently needed as chauffeurs. Gareth was supreme here, even driving to Ealing and back in a day for Bethan's clarinet lesson.

During the two years before the accident, when Gareth was Professor of Education at Aberystwyth, the extent of his independence grew, both professionally and domestically. He spent much of the week away from home, based in our small flat quite near his college. He came back to Pennard whenever possible, certainly at weekends and vacations, but also as a more convenient route to, for instance, Cardiff or London. However, when at the flat, for the first time in his life he lived alone, with complete freedom to organise his time to suit himself. It is true he hated this isolation from the family, especially going back to emptiness in the evenings, but he was determined not to be the oft-maligned academic who lives far from his university and puts in the absolute minimum time there. In his second year at Aberystwyth, as head of department, he needed to be on site all weekdays, unless away at significant meetings or conferences.

Gareth had been reluctant to take charge of the department, finding his research post well-nigh perfect, but eventually allowed himself to be persuaded. He took pride in introducing a more democratic style of leadership than was hitherto in operation, everyone having responsibility for a particular aspect of the work. Clearly he was by no means without advice from his staff or others in the college hierarchy, but ultimately it was up to him to see the department prospered. His policies were put into practice and he masterminded the operations. There was obviously a certain satisfaction for Gareth in taking decisions which gradually shaped the education section according to his own ideals. However, this degree of independence in connection with matters of importance, which often also involved large amounts of money, was inevitably very demanding. By the end of this year in office Gareth, normally very slim, had lost weight and looked tired.

At least Gareth's lecturing load was substantially reduced during this last year – not more than six hours a week. He did find even this limited contact with students a welcome relief from the burden of administration which occupied most of his day. All mail addressed to the head of department was subjected to a preliminary sifting by the administrative officer and anything requiring Gareth's attention brought to his room. There was always a pile of this correspondence to greet him in the morning and to keep him prisoner for long hours. He might, for instance, reply to the queries of research students; to requests for consideration for jobs or for references; to internal memos about finance; or to a whole host of matters relating to students on teaching practice – especially those few who were having problems. However much delegation he managed, and it was considerable, there was always a wealth of paper left to ensure that academic research receded into the distance. Sometimes he would ring home in the evening complaining he had only just cleared his desk, admitting metaphorically to be running as fast as he could, only to stand still. Yet since he knew any backlog would become more and more difficult to cope with, there was no option but the struggle to keep up. Managerial decisions were required and it was up to him to make them.

Not only was Gareth a slave to paper; he also maintained an open-door policy for staff. He believed very strongly that a head of department should always be available for consultation at the shortest possible notice – and usually immediately. Given the complex nature of their work, it wasn't surprising that each day Gareth would receive several visits about teaching loads, research grants, articles to be submitted, and problems about students or rooms or books or resources. Some of these queries could be answered at once, but in many cases a longer term strategy was required to resolve the underlying difficulty – in these cases Gareth would stick yet another post-it note on the outside of his word processor to act as a reminder. Now and again, he was just a shoulder to cry on.

Perhaps the most worrying decisions Gareth had to make were those to do with the financial crisis experienced by universities since the 1980s. Education departments had unique additional difficulties thrust upon them in the early 1990s when the government forced them to pay schools for their part in training college-based students when on teaching practice. Gareth wondered if it was possible to keep his department solvent when passing on a third of student revenue in this way. The problem was felt right across Wales and England, so Gareth attended national conferences convened to decide on a common strategy to cope with such swingeing cuts in funding. He was also involved in negotiations with all the schools in which Aberystwyth students had their teaching practice – determining the amount of money to be paid and formalising precisely what they must do to earn this sum.

This incredible pressure on the budget of education departments had all sorts of undesirable knock-on effects and Gareth had endless meetings with staff and students to work out the detailed implications. For instance, to save money, many staff were given only short-term contracts. This meant constant uncertainty for them and tension for Gareth who had to be the link between them and the finance office. Also there had to be cuts in the funding given to students to help pay for their transport and, where necessary, lodgings, when on teaching practice sometimes quite distant from Aberystwyth. Once again it was only Gareth, as head of department, who could take responsibility for forging a delicate balance between all these factors and, at the same time, run a unified and contented department.

At a very much simpler level, Gareth would make minor decisions about, for instance, where and when he took much needed breaks during his working day. There was no refectory, so at mid-morning he chose between a trip downstairs to the machine which dispensed grim coffee or undrinkable tea, and an expedition down one set of stairs, across the quad and up an uncountable number of stone steps to the top of the tower on the other side of the building, where the staff could make their own tea or coffee. Since this was the Aberystwyth version of Everest, the room was never densely populated and Gareth wasn't convinced new members of staff would ever find it. At lunch time the choice was between a profusion of cafés and sandwich bars, entirely fitting for a town which is a seaside resort. Most members of the education department ended up in the Cabin café, secure in the knowledge that there they would find some colleagues to engage in conversation. By five o'clock another sanity-saving break was called for – and time to think whether or not to take a customary stroll along the sea front. A final serious matter of choice would be whether to call in a pizza restaurant or collect a takeaway meal! That the former was the most usual choice is shown by Gareth's regular, free top-up of wine and the use of the owner's *Daily Mail*.

The ability to make such ordinary choices is as much part of the concept of independence as is Gareth's running of his department. Yet there is another level of independence beyond the ones I have mentioned and which is never visible until it is challenged. The 'small' matters of when to get up, washing and dressing oneself –

even the freedom to go to the lavatory – are taken for granted, but become overwhelmingly significant when obstacles arise which prevent their being carried out with ease. Again, there is the ability to get to places without difficulty; to run out to the car and get in with no thought of how this is achieved; to drive as a simple and natural operation; park with no consideration of how to get out of the vehicle; walk freely along any pavement or road; and have immediate access to any building. Gareth would hurry through the town, step down into Old College and climb the stone stairs to his room, performing these actions as spontaneously and unthinkingly as his breathing used to be.

There can be no doubt that until his accident Gareth could, to a large extent, truly be described as independent. The knowledge of what he was before the accident makes the contrast with the present more poignant, indeed tragic. It is no coincidence that through all his more or less constant presence in Old College over two years, he saw no one in a wheelchair.

7

Moving Forward

Rookwood, the rehabilitation centre, is a long, low, rambling building added on to a much taller house that was built in 1866. It had been taken over in 1918 as a convalescent home for servicemen injured in the second World War. Later it became a kind of hospital, specialising in spinally-injured, brain-damaged and stroke-affected patients. Equivalent to Stoke Mandeville in England, it is one of the very few centres for those who have broken their neck or back. In recent years it has often been rumoured that it is to be closed, which would be a real tragedy for the many disabled people living within a huge radius of the place.

I closely followed the ambulance on the fairly complex route from CRI – my mind alternating between dread and hope. On arrival Gareth was driven straight up to the main door whilst Bethan and I, with some difficulty, found a space in the crowded visitors' parking area. As we hurried to find the way to Gareth, we had a vague impression of several wheelchair users moving quite independently about the level grounds, apparently enjoying the fine summer's day. We also noticed small groups of people relaxing in the seats scattered around the lawns as they chatted to inmates. At once we were getting accustomed to an environment in which being unable to walk was quite an ordinary feature of life.

As we reached the building, yet another person in a wheelchair guided himself through the automatically-opening doors and down the gentle slope. He smiled at us and moved off at speed. Inside we stopped at the porters' office and, on asking for Gareth, were directed towards ward six. Hesitantly we walked along the passage which led first of all to a small space that was in fact the intersection of a few corridors. Here we took note of a shop, seemingly staffed by volunteers, selling sweets, crisps, drinks, magazines and second-hand books. Glancing around briefly, we saw a hot-drinks machine and a few chairs for visitors or for patients who could walk. A fish tank and reproductions on the walls completed what was clearly meant to be a pleasant, recreational place. However this was not the time to fully appreciate the provision of such amenities.

We followed the corridor down a gradual but extended slope past various treatment rooms and found ourselves facing the narrow entrance to ward six. In spite of all our CRI experiences, Bethan and I both felt apprehensive as we glimpsed the seething world beyond, but there was nothing to be done apart from squaring our shoulders and advancing. The areas containing beds were all to the right, so without needing to seem inquisitive by staring at these, we were able to continue straight to a longish counter. This was the centre for the nurses and someone was usually sitting here on duty, day and night. A friendly nurse asked if she could help and took us to a day room to wait while Gareth was with a doctor.

We were so relieved to sense the relaxed atmosphere of

the place. Some patients in wheelchairs were watching television and, as Bethan and I sat down in the nearest chairs, a bed was pushed in by nurses so that someone could have a 'secret' cigarette. The bed virtually filled the whole room, but no one minded and it was obviously a not-unusual occurrence. It looked as if the *raison d'être* of this place was going to be understanding, and there was no need to fear a rigid, disciplined regime. Hot cups of tea and coffee quickly appeared for Bethan and me, again a reassuring act of kindness. However, we couldn't fail to see a disabled lavatory and a large number of empty wheelchairs of every shape and size. Whatever the cheerful surface of the room, this physical equipment – and obviously much more so the existence of so many disabled people – told a different story.

I thought conversation might be strained in this context, but not a bit of it. 'Why are you here? Who are you visiting?' were the first of many spontaneous questions. By the time Bethan, with some additions from me, had said a little of Gareth's accident and condition we were accepted as part of the furniture. There were about six patients in the room, and I think that each had been spinally-injured through an unlucky, unique occurrence which had marred their life, probably for ever. The inevitable subjects of conversation were a comparison of accidents, levels of spinal break, specific problems encountered and ways of coping with these. Each case was different. Some people were in the early stages of rehabilitation, some were long resigned to the permanence of their condition, whilst some were actually showing slight improvement. We were deluged with information brought out afresh for our benefit, but clearly also a permanent source of fascination for the rest of the patients. All this was bewildering and upsetting. Underneath the friendliness and brave faces we sensed something of the struggle to cope with disability. As we had witnessed terrible suffering of patients and their families in CRI, so now we saw people living not so much with the prospect of death, but with ongoing tragedy. How would this relate to Gareth and the rest of us?

Before long the patients in the bed and wheelchairs were called back to the ward for some reason. Bethan was getting restless at having no news of her father and decided to explore a little. I was alone in the day room when a youngish, good-looking man came in, propelling his wheelchair with rapidity and ease. He told me that he was only here for a few days recuperating after a minor bladder operation. After some preliminaries he allowed what I soon learned to be his habitual sadness to settle over his features, and he confided that no one wanted him to go home. He said that it would only mean more work for his wife and that he could no longer keep his two boys in order. They wouldn't listen if he told them off, only laughed at a safe distance. 'What can I do for any of them?' he asked and answered himself, 'Nothing'. I was shocked at this glimpse of an unhappy world in which he would grow more bitter with age, and in which there seemed to be no solutions to the problems. Previously he had earned a reasonable wage; now he only had the benefits given to disabled people resulting in a substantial drop in the family's standard of living. This in itself was hard enough for his wife and boys to accept, without all the physical restrictions. I tried to convince him that of course he was welcome at home, whatever was said in times of stress, but with all his knowledge of the situation he could only answer bitterly, 'They would be better off without me.' I so wanted to comfort him, but what could I say? He was taken home by ambulance a few days later and I never saw him again. His words, however, made a lasting impression on me, adding additional sombre depth to my understanding of the struggle with disability.

I seemed to have been in the day room for a very long time and was delighted when Bethan burst in saying we could now see Gareth. He lay in the bed nearest to the nurses' counter so that, as the latest admission, they could keep an eye on him. He didn't actually speak to us at once because he was exchanging pleasantries with a nurse in Welsh! Eventually we heard all about the thorough examination given him by an impressive Dr Grove. She came over to introduce herself and to give us some idea of the Rookwood regime. It seems that there was a spinal injuries consultant who was involved in research, and one other doctor who helped to run ward six. Dr Grove would be coming into daily contact with her patients, making her ward round at about ten o'clock and taking all major decisions with regard to treatment. She looked surprisingly young to have this enormous responsibility and was not an obvious authority figure, being slight with short, curly, brown hair. Her flat shoes and very long, unbuttoned, white coat made her look shorter and younger still. However she had a firm way of speaking which suggested she would brook no opposition. I found her intimidating, but was encouraged by the confidence she inspired.

Lying in bed, Gareth did not look any different from how he was in CRI. He did seem to have made the transition well and was taking an eager interest in his new surroundings. I was relieved to see the oxygen supply behind his bed, though thus far it hadn't been needed – indeed he wouldn't have been brought to Rookwood if he wasn't expected to be able to breathe independently. However he was, as ever, painfully conscious of the fact that he still could only move his head and arms. The same questions which had tormented us for seven long weeks were causing us misery now. Gareth had tried to get Dr Grove to say whether she thought he would get better, or even to give him some idea of the percentage of people with his particular injury who did recover. Wisely, perhaps, she refused to be drawn: 'I'm not a betting man' was how she put it! In spite of this guarded reply, within the family we emphasised the curative, rather than the rehabilitation side of Rookwood. We put our faith in the combined expertise of the medical staff. Surely they would be able to restore the disrupted nerve patterns – they simply had to!

All through this first day Gareth couldn't rest from his search to find out more about the techniques that would be employed to cure him. He pestered nurses and fellow patients for information whenever they came in range of his bed. Try as he might, he found no one who referred to anything but physiotherapy. This was a major disappointment as we had hoped for all sorts of exciting approaches to the paralysis, each one bringing a new wave of hope. The probability that no other treatment existed did nothing to relieve Gareth's obsession with the loss of fine movement in his hands. It was terrible not to be able to stand or walk; but not to be able to turn pages, to write, even to dress or feed himself, was certain descent into misery and uselessness. How could he earn money so we could live? How could Bethan and Matthew complete their education?

This mental agony was compounded by the well-meant suggestion from Dr Grove that Gareth should no longer think of himself as ill, since this was a misnomer. He must learn to accept the label 'disabled'. This was something the whole family still desperately rebelled against, whether rationally or not. It ruled out the hope of recovery and the return to security, making more horribly urgent his natural constant reversion to matters of organisation and finance. He had looked ahead, planned for a retirement in relative comfort with the children well established in their careers. And now for this to happen! It is impossible to over-emphasise what a disaster this was to him, the man who had covered every eventuality.

Despite these worries, by the end of this day Gareth had physically become well established in his new surroundings. Between us, we had more or less gathered the extent of the ward. There seemed to be separate male and female areas, and I think, two single rooms. Perhaps there would be twenty patients on the whole ward. Many of these were bedridden, so only those in neighbouring beds or in wheelchairs could introduce themselves to Gareth. Bethan and I smiled rather sadly to see a repetition of the conversation we had taken part in when first in the day room. Gareth too was bewildered by the masses of detail about accidents, breaks in the spinal cord and resulting problems. But at least he felt surrounded by fellow sufferers who understood his predicament. The nurses were also friendly, especially the one who insisted on speaking in Welsh to Gareth. In this place his condition did not make him feel conspicuous; quite the contrary. He was simply one of the many spinally-injured patients. Bethan and I also felt comfortable here. Friends and relatives were visiting other patients and we were all accepted quite naturally. There seemed no specific end to visiting hours or limits to the number of visitors. We took it in turns to give Gareth his food and cups of tea. This helped the nurses a bit, as part of their job was to spoon-feed quite a large number of patients and give them drinks through a straw. For a long time we were always given drinks whenever the patients had them, but after a crisis when the supplies of coffee and tea dwindled alarmingly, there was a strict ban on treating visitors! Most of the time we could only sit, sharing observations about our new environment and bolstering each other's morale. Towards evening we were offered a bed in the old house just for one night and gratefully accepted. After that we would have to drive from Pennard daily.

That night both Bethan and I slept instantly and heavily, probably as a result of nervous exhaustion. Next morning after a sumptuous breakfast of crisps, chocolate and drinks from the machine, we hastened to ward six. A scene of great activity met our eyes and we were politely requested to wait in the day room until the ward was sorted out. It was not something I had thought about before, but getting twenty disabled people washed and dressed clearly required considerable time and effort. Then it was time to serve breakfast and I was surprised to see this was done by the nurses rather than some sort of orderly. At ten, Dr Grove made her round of the ward, and only after that could treatment of any sort begin. Bethan and I were allowed to sit by Gareth at this stage and were listening with pleasure to his account of an uncomplicated night when a physiotherapist arrived.

We had grown accustomed to seeing Gareth's hands being manipulated in CRI and now Ann, a member of another team of physiotherapists, sat at his bedside and started to curve the hands around to form a fist. We had known from the very beginning that the left hand was malleable and, at rest, would form a natural-looking shape. The right one remained stiff, with the fingers pointing straight out and they could not be bent round. Oddly enough the more flexible one was totally insentient, whilst there was a flicker of feeling in the fore-finger of the rigid hand. Ann explained that the joints of the right hand had become inflamed, so Gareth was put on anti-inflammatory tablets. The muscles between the thumb and palm of each hand were completely wasted, leaving a sad sort of hollow. The possibility of his ever grasping a pen looked infinitely remote.

Ann taught the whole family how to manipulate Gareth's hands and we worked away with vigour whenever we were just sitting together, starting at once. She also mentioned that light tapping could sometimes get the nerves moving, so we tapped and bent for hours at a time. If it wasn't the hi-tech approach we had anticipated, it was wonderful to feel each of us was contributing to a possible cure. Occasionally one of us would say 'Try to move your thumb' or 'Can you bend this finger at all? – Try!' Never were hands so observed. Sometimes there would seem to be a tiny quiver in the little finger of the left hand and we would all get excited and optimistic. Sometimes one or other of the thumbs would move a scarcely-discernible amount. One day

Gareth discovered he could slightly twitch the top section of the middle finger of his right hand. Clearly it was voluntary movement, not spasm, so we thought it highly significant. Now it seems pitiful to think of the castles we built on these slightest of foundations. Whenever we brought such minor discoveries to the attention of the next physiotherapist, he or she would be only cautiously optimistic. It could be the start of a substantial recovery, though the odds weren't big. How frantically we attacked these hands! (The family efforts continued for years, until I hurt my hands, and after two separate 'hammer-thumb' operations, we decided that the family needed at least one pair of functional hands to survive and that we had better look after mine.)

We had been told on our arrival at Rookwood that Gareth would be kept in bed under observation for a few days. At some point in the morning of the second day I had gone briefly in search of some information, leaving Bethan with her father. When I returned, what was my amazement at seeing his bed empty and Gareth next to it sitting in a wheelchair! Bethan was pleased to see my surprised delight. My imagination had never ventured beyond an image of him propped up in an armchair, and never thought he could even sit completely upright. In CRI he had been slowly levered upwards, at no point approaching the vertical. To overcome his very low blood pressure, the Rookwood nurses had bound a tight, elasticated 'corset' round his middle and wound 'blue-line' bandages round the full extent of his legs. (They normally used support stockings but Gareth's legs were so pitifully thin that the smallest size was loose on him.) Even then he kept feeling faint and his vision would start to break up. Bethan had been taught what to do when this happened and she explained it to me. The first thing was to put the brakes on, then tilt the chair backwards, by putting a foot on one of two projecting rods low down its back. It could recline to the horizontal if necessary and the position held until he began to feel better. Then it was a question of trial and error until his condition stabilised for a short while.

The ward was always warm and Gareth was dressed in a pair of pyjamas – the only clothes he possessed that he could wear now without marking his skin. He looked nearer his usual self than at any time since the accident, apart from the plaster covering the 'trache' hole. Most important he was smiling broadly. It is strange that none of us seemed to consider the more negative associations of the concept of a wheelchair, the ideas of disability and deviation from normality. At the time it just was a sign of progress, the beginning of mobility, and anyway, there was nothing to say he wouldn't relinquish it for crutches later. When lying paralysed in bed, with one's world restricted to the confines of a bed, struggling around on crutches looks to be an idyllic option. Cheerfully I asked for, and was granted, permission for the two of us to push Gareth out of the ward and a little way along the corridor. Bethan and I felt nervous at the thought of being out of the sight of nurses, but glad too. For the first time in months he was considered well enough to be away from a hospital ward. Before long, we thought, we could take him up to the shop area and even explore the grounds on fine days – what an expedition this would be in our new circumstances!

We passed Dr Grove on the way out of the ward and

she smiled at our obvious elation, 'The sooner we could get him into a wheelchair, the better for him', she said, 'but it won't be for long because we've got to watch his skin. It'll be longer each time.' Slowly Bethan started to push up the slight incline. Every couple of yards Gareth said, 'Stop. My vision's going!' and Bethan would tilt the chair right back until his blood pressure rose again. Then we set off once more. We didn't get far this first time, but it was a landmark of sorts. Shortly after we reached the ward again, two nurses lifted a regretful Gareth into bed. His skin had reddened alarmingly and he was told that he wouldn't be allowed up again until all signs of red had vanished. The rule was, 'If it's red, stay in bed!'

Later that day Gareth had his second visit to a wheelchair. This time it was made clear to him that he was not going to sit like a lump of lead and be pushed around – far from it. An occupational therapist appeared from nowhere bearing a pair of 'driving gloves'. These were fingerless, leather strips, having velcro fastening, and with the palm area strengthened and covered with a layer of rubber for gripping. Without these the skin would become blistered and painful after a very short time of pushing the chair wheels round. To his utter amazement and trepidation this was what Gareth was required to do! Typically, he made sure he could reach and just about manipulate the brakes before starting. Then gingerly he positioned his hands on the large inner wheels and got the idea of propelling himself immediately. The trouble was that he was so weak he could hardly move at all. The ward itself was flat, but there were always obstacles to avoid in the shape of other wheelchairs, the large moveable telephone with its long black lead to go over, the tea or tablet trolleys, and hoists. Gareth found changing direction completely exhausting, but still he did have some freedom of choice as to where he went, even if it was limited to which patient he wanted to visit. This was the very first tiny step towards any kind of post-accident independence.

The biggest physical challenge facing ward six patients was the long, sloping corridor up to the visitors' area. It was not steep and the surface was smooth, but the problem was to find the strength to go the whole way without the ignominy of rolling down again backwards, crashing into other wheelchair users. The chairs' brakes were long metal levers which had to be pulled or pushed to operate – no real trouble on the flat as Gareth had found, but tricky when using your hands to try to keep the chair in position on a slope. I don't think Gareth ever made that whole journey unaided. Certainly on this first time of pushing himself, he gladly relinquished control as soon as he was out of sight of the ward. Bethan and I took it in turn to push, glancing around guiltily in case we were caught. We reached the small recreational area at the top of the corridor and celebrated with drinks from the machine.

From then on the wheelchair became an accepted part of daily routine. Straight after breakfast Gareth would be lifted into it and, apart from the skin-care breaks, would be in it all day. I vividly remember hearing a fellow patient being asked, 'Don't you feel trapped in your wheelchair?' and his response: 'No – I feel trapped when I'm not in it'. I could see what he meant. Where would he, or Gareth for that matter, be without it?

With our fresh interest in wheelchairs we began to be

aware of a vast array of different types. Gareth pointed out that the way different people propel their chairs is one of the surest indicators of their condition. The basic manual chair, like the one Gareth had been lent, was mainly for those who had lost the use of their legs but had some upper-body control and strength. We saw a couple of very lightweight, sporting models, the sort you see in wheelchair races and they were always occupied by athletic types, usually with dramatic contrast between wonderfully muscular arms and helpless legs. We were told that some of these supremely fit people played wheelchair rugby, bending low from the waist to pick up the ball, skilfully outmanoeuvring their opponents and mostly avoiding collisions – we could only marvel. Then we noticed that electrically-controlled chairs were used by patients with very restricted movement of hands and arms, because they would have difficulty using a manual chair. Gareth could see that these were usually operated by a joystick attached to the arm of the chair and could be used with little or no finger movement, the palm steering by pushing the knob in different directions. We saw examples of these that had been engineered to suit the needs of individuals in almost unbelievably intricate ways. He rather fancied such an effortless way of moving as it took all his strength to creep a few yards. However he was firmly told that a manual chair was much better for his heart and general health. There was no choice anyway at this stage, so he was resigned to it. It was good to be told that the Welsh Office, now the Welsh Assembly, provided free 'push-along' chairs – though electric chairs had to be bought privately unless absolutely necessary.

The day after Gareth's introduction to a wheelchair we

welcomed Matthew back from Switzerland. Instead of going straight home he left the train at Cardiff and took a taxi to Rookwood. His lively stories of the course and concerts reminded the rest of us that there was a different world outside the hospital. This did us good, but it must have been a terrible shock for Matthew to see his father's desperate efforts to move a little way across the ward. Yet he had to recognise it was progress, better than seeing him lying in bed – only how he must have longed on his return to witness some lessening of the paralysis, some true recovery. At least he joined the family in an environment where we were welcomed, and here he could see his father regularly, instead of coping with the gnawing worry which kept him company when he was away.

Life took on a regular pattern for the rest of August and the first part of September. Each day I would drive either Bethan or Matthew, usually both, to Rookwood. I timed the forty-five mile journey for us to arrive a bit before two o'clock, the hospital staff finding that visitors tended to get in the way of the patients' full morning time-table. We would get back to Pennard after ten at night, physically and mentally exhausted. At weekends we could be with Gareth as early as we liked, knowing we were not interrupting a routine. This existence, with the whole family spending virtually all their waking hours in the hospital, couldn't go on for ever. Matthew started his second sixth form year in Gorseinon College, whilst Bethan began her MA course at Bristol University. Terrified of penury, Gareth and I decided that I must return to work on a part-time basis. My headmaster, as helpful as ever, arranged for me to teach five mornings a week.

I tried my hardest to ensure that Gareth wouldn't suffer because of these changes. During the week I would finish school at twelve, then drive up to Cardiff, stopping to eat sandwiches on the way. I wouldn't leave Rookwood until late evening. Life was greatly changed for Matthew. Previously I was almost always around to prepare meals and just to be available in what I like to think was a warm, supportive home. Now he came home to silence until past ten. Weekends were enlivened by two long hospital visits in which he tried to do his homework or musical composition – in an atmosphere far from congenial to study. He insisted on coming, however, right through that term. On 16 September he celebrated his eighteenth birthday by coming from Gorseinon College to Rookwood by bus. Bethan too, travelled down from Bristol whenever she could on Saturdays or Sundays. Our main aim was to have at least one member of the family with Gareth as much as possible. It was obvious how forlorn he was on his own. He couldn't even read to pass the time, since he could neither hold a book nor turn pages. I sometimes left a newspaper on the edge of the bed in his line of vision, but he usually stopped me because it was too frustrating for him not to be able to manage it. Basically he could only sit in his wheelchair thinking anything but cheerful thoughts. He told me that the worst time was from when I left for the night until bedtime. On the other hand, he looked forward to my appearance in the early afternoon. If he was in the ward I would just catch a glimpse of the impassive, hopeless body language before it changed as he saw me.

However it was only when treatment for the day was over that the emptiness and sadness were pre-eminent.

Apart from visits from Dr Grove and other staff, at least one hour of each weekday morning was spent on his recovery programme. Gareth was desperate for this to start and I heard how on the first morning, about a fortnight after admission, he tried to chivvy the nurses to hasten his dressing and washing – only with difficulty conveying his sense of urgency and anticipation. He was, however, ready by half past ten when the physiotherapists came to collect him. They wheeled him across the long tarmac courtyard and into the gym. Pausing only to switch on Radio 2, they introduced Gareth to weight training, hopefully the means of developing his feeble biceps and triceps. Basically all the apparatus boiled down to straight steel bars to be gripped and pulled through a system of pulleys to lift variable weights. The trouble was that Gareth had no grip. Nothing daunted, the physios produced heavy-duty gloves which were strapped around his wrists and tied to the bar so that his arms were pulling the bar. These were ingenious, but not that effective. The saddest part of Gareth's narrative was that by the end of the session his hands had stiffened and swollen. He fervently, if not optimistically, wished all his hopes wouldn't be so speedily dashed.

The next afternoon I found an equally dejected Gareth. That morning he had experienced his first 'games' session which alternated with the weight training. The activities were pursued with the best possible motives by the physiotherapy staff who were almost invariably interested, sympathetic and constructive. First Gareth tried table tennis and he could hit the ball if it chanced within reach of his chair, but the static position and having a bat strapped to his wrist, was a pretty sad reminder of things past – he had been a reasonably good player. Skittles seemed to him to be completely pointless amongst participants who couldn't grasp the ball – the element of competitiveness on which the game depends simply didn't exist. Worst of all was snooker. We had a three-quarters size table at home and Gareth was the undoubted family champion – the result of a misspent youth! Now someone bridged for him and all he could do was push the end of a cue with both hands. Throughout the whole session there were the occasional flashes of achievement, but also a permanent agonising recollection of the sheer fun of physical activities – now probably lost for ever.

All I wanted to do was to lighten this perfectly rationally-based dejection. But how was that possible? I knew that the first afternoon part of Gareth's programme would start as soon as the physios were ready for him. I was encouraged to go with him and devoutly hoped it would be cheering. Soon we were in a large gym with acres of windows, the coldest room in a hot hospital. It was full of contraptions designed either to extend or make the most of limited mobility. For instance, there was a standing frame clamping a spinally-injured patient in an upright position in order to stimulate natural blood flow and allow organs to resume their normal positions. Gareth was lifted onto a tilt-table which allowed him to be very slowly brought to the vertical through measurable angles. It was wonderful to be standing again, in spite of all the artificial means to achieve it. Unfortunately after a very few minutes he started to feel faint and was hastily brought down and given an ephedrine tablet! Another patient who was making slow progress towards being able to walk again was put in a waist high supporting frame and struggled to put one foot in front of the other. Yet another was on a treadmill for the same purpose. Gareth and the others who were less fortunate were torn between delight for their fellows and downright envy that they would ultimately join the world of the walking.

While he waited for the tablet to take effect, about twenty minutes, Gareth was warmly wrapped up in what turned out to be his most important piece of learning equipment. It was a very large, flat, 'bed' which was about wheelchair height and was covered in some sort of blue, waterproof fabric. When he felt more human, the physios began by teaching him exercises to strengthen his hopelessly weak arms. Then he was shown how to fling both his arms vigorously to one side in the hope of gaining a momentum which would turn his whole body over that way. He simply couldn't do it and at first wondered why it should matter. Firmly he was told that it is vital that he should be able to change his position in the night, as part of the campaign against bed sores. Poor Gareth thrashed around like a stranded fish, feeling miserable and cold. He knew he could never do it, not with a rigid spondylitis-fused spine. However, he made no headway in communicating this to the physiotherapists. This was the first occasion of the only criticism he ever made of the Rookwood regime, namely that treatment occasionally tended to be prescribed on the basis of stereotypes, rather than on consideration of individual differences. He felt he would be seen as not putting in enough effort to turn over, and not that on purely physical grounds he was an exception to the rule.

Feeling an utter failure, Gareth was put back in his chair and taken over to a recreational area where ball games were devised to increase dexterity and sharpen reactions. He was placed at one end of a long table and given a large soft ball to roll to an elderly lady at the other end. There was nothing intrinsically wrong with the activity, but here was someone who had once played cricket for Swansea University, rolling a child's ball along a table to a dear old lady, not like some condescending politician in an old people's home, but on equal terms. This put the final seal of misery on the first day of Gareth's programme. I wheeled him back to the ward and to a very long evening where we went over and over what had happened, searching for something that could be recalled with happiness.

One day, shortly after this, an occupational therapist appeared in ward six bearing a board about two feet long and nine inches wide. It was laminated on one side, wooden on the other, and the edges were rounded. The whole thing was perfectly smooth. 'Take this to your physio session this afternoon,' she said. We did just this and were told it was a sliding board which could be used to transfer Gareth from bed to chair without any lifting. It seemed far too simple an object for such a major function and we watched eagerly. He was parked right next to the large bed and the wheelchair arm on that side was removed, as were the footplates. The board was gently wedged underneath Gareth by tipping him to one side, the other end resting on the bed. He could then use his hands, in spite of having no gripping power, to push himself along the board and fall backwards onto the bed. It was trickier the other way because he had to be propped up on the edge of the bed and held steady, while the chair was manoeuvred into the exact position for the end of the board to rest on it securely. Still, even this looked straightforward enough when carried out by experts, but I was alarmed when told to do it the following day! For one thing his feet could get caught in the wheels. Much more important, having no sense of balance, he could end up on the floor. He had to lean forward with his head on my shoulder and be stopped falling in any other direction. I kept a tight grasp of the waistband of his tracksuit bottoms, ready to take his weight if necessary. It did work, though I was shaking for quite a while afterwards. We felt something had been achieved that day and began to see his programme in a more positive light.

As far as Gareth and I were concerned, the aim of these physiotherapy activities was to teach us how best to cope with what was assumed to be permanent, severe disability. While immersed in them, problems for the most part were purely practical. When back in the ward we had at least five hours to reflect on what we had done and why. There is little that appears more basic than getting in and out of bed or changing position through the night. Would the life for which we were being prepared be nothing more than a physical struggle to stay alive? The afternoon sessions implicitly supported 'think of yourself as disabled' – and perhaps the balance between hope and despair was shifting in favour of the latter. The trouble was that our concept of a disabled existence was so desperately limited that it seemed worthless. Alongside the prayer, 'Please let him get better, back to security and happiness', we needed also to ask for strength to make the best of how things might remain, whatever the cost and however catastrophic. Perhaps we were beginning to grope in a confused and halting way towards the latter, as the former became more and more unlikely. Were we all being rehabilitated?

Interlude

Spain – Brittany Ferries (1996/7)

A thin, off-white cat watched hungrily as a relaxed family in holiday mood awaited the meat sizzling on the barbecue. Only one of the party was a carnivore and the vegetarian option gently simmered in the oven. At length everyone ate with enthusiasm, relishing the warmth of the late Spanish evening. The cat's patience was rewarded and soon he curled up nearby to sleep off the effects of the good food. After a few drinks and a game of Scrabble, the people followed suit. On opening the door next morning, the first thing to be seen was the same cat enthusiastically licking the grill of the barbecue! Somehow cooking *al fresco* seemed substantially less attractive and the vegetarians had a not-to-be-missed opportunity for mirth! But could anything really matter when the whole business of these lazy days was to seek out the best sources of enjoyment?

Our main motivation since the accident has been to live as near as possible to a 'normal' life. This involves a traditional family holiday and, in a lasting testimonial to their good nature, Bethan and Matthew continue whenever possible to come with us. (They insist it is for their enjoyment but know all too well how difficult it can be for us on our own. It only takes, for instance, a bed to be a few inches too low, a door to be too narrow, a car to break down or me to be ill, for us to be in trouble. Anything wrong with Gareth would mean disaster on a massive scale.) A year after our totally depressing Motor Rail experience, we opted for the twenty-four-hour sea crossing from Plymouth to Santander. After searching through piles of holiday brochures, I discovered a delightful looking house in Catalonia with easy access for the wheelchair, a ground floor bedroom and a swimming pool (albeit small and kidney-shaped). It shouldn't be too hard a journey if we used the Spanish motorways and spent a night in an hotel half way between the ferry and our destination.

The big questions for us were whether the wheelchair could get on the ship and whether there was a suitable cabin. Gareth rang Brittany Ferries and was assured that there were two disabled cabins conveniently placed near the lifts; also that the latter were certainly big enough for any wheelchair plus attendant. He asked for the actual dimensions of the lifts and, upon receiving them, thought them small. With the previous year's false promises ever present in our minds, we were still doubtful. Eventually we were offered a chance to try the ship out between unloading and re-loading at Plymouth. This was such a helpful suggestion that we gratefully accepted at once, and went on to book a room in a Campanile hotel quite near the port (since all the reasonably-priced hotels in this chain are identical, with disabled rooms and good access). The extra expense would, we were sure, be more than compensated by our peace of mind.

The journey was uneventful, the night comfortable, and we presented ourselves at the ferry terminal the following morning. A lady conducted us through a strange maze of narrow streets and corridors to a room with basic refreshment facilities and asked us to wait there until the ship was empty. (Obviously we couldn't use the normal passenger routes since they would be full.) We drank tea and coffee and were just beginning to wonder if we'd been forgotten, when our guide returned and took us to the lifts. Again we followed a tortuous but level route. Gareth was very relieved to see the size of the lifts; much larger that the measurements he thought he'd been given. We reached the appropriate deck and just around a corner was an excellently-designed disabled cabin. There was plenty of room for Gareth to manoeuvre his chair, a good-sized bathroom (for a ship!), and two single beds. I would be able to transfer Gareth to the more solid one of these. Thanks to the exceptional kindness of Brittany Ferries we returned home very happy and could look forward to the holiday with confidence.

None of the family could speak any Spanish and with Gareth in his condition, communication can sometimes be vital. To this end I decided to take an elementary course which was held in our local school. With no particular aptitude for languages and a realistic assessment of my probable progress, I didn't work very hard. However, I could for instance ask the way, even if there was little hope of my understanding the answer! After making this limited effort, I was rather daunted to find that Catalan was spoken in Catalonia and it was different from Castilian, the language I was learning. There could even be hostility, I was told, between those speaking the two languages. As it turned out, Matthew's excellent Italian was our most helpful tool because of the similarities between this and Spanish. Also he and Bethan listened to

Spanish tapes whilst lounging by the pool and learnt far more in a week than I had in a year!

As the holiday drew nearer, I began to worry about the drive. Since my early twenties I had experienced occasional back pain. The amount of physical effort needed on a daily basis since the accident had substantially worsened the condition. Now not only was the pain severe, but it had spread to my legs, especially the right one. Sometimes, as I drove, it got stuck in a fixed position and had to be lifted using my hands. I had visions of being unable to continue at some point halfway through Spain and having somehow to get a driver to take us home at once. We also had a recurrent but totally unpredictable problem with our adapted Chrysler van. About once or twice a year the engine would turn over as usual when the ignition was switched on, but would cut out as soon as it was put in the drive position. (Once when this happened, we had to call out the AA in the middle of a busy London street.) The diagnostic computer in the local Chrysler garage failed to find the fault, so for ages we waited in suspense every time the car was started. A breakdown anywhere was potentially dangerous for Gareth, but suppose the engine wouldn't keep running when we tried to continue our journey after a break in a Spanish lay-by? It would be very hot, obviously the air-conditioning wouldn't work, Gareth would get dehydrated and we wouldn't be able to explain the problem . . . Living with disability is always living on a knife edge, and confronting possible disasters is essential to being able to cope should they occur. It's also incredibly discouraging and completely rules out carefree enjoyment.

When the holiday time arrived, we found out that most

of our worries had been in vain. Getting on to the ferry was straightforward. In fact, as with the shorter channel crossings, disabled people are given special treatment, their vehicles being given a particular lane and either being loaded first or last. The van had an automatically-operated sliding door on the right-hand side, opening to reveal a ramp which was lowered using the same control. We had explained that Gareth needed access to a lift from that side and were waved into a perfect position. It is true there was the usual wait and scramble before we actually boarded the lift, but Bethan and Matthew had gone ahead and taken over a pleasant corner of the central lounge very near our cabin. Their own cabin wasn't far away and soon the luggage was stored and we were relaxing with books and newspapers. There was a plethora of entertainment aboard, including a swimming pool and a cinema, though not much that was suitable for us. We only attempted a travel talk about Spain but the room was so crowded that the wheelchair couldn't get in. Various eating places were provided but, since none of us felt quite right in spite of the calmness of the sea, we only ate in a café on our deck. The time passed pleasantly. Our main topic of conversation was the choice of a subject matter for a musical Bethan and Matthew were writing – and weird and wonderful were some of the suggestions. (Throughout the holiday there was tremendous creative activity; both composed tunes, Bethan in particular wrote lyrics and Matthew orchestrated. The result was a two-hour musical, 'Slingshot!', which was finally performed at Warwick University Arts Centre and most enthusiastically received.)

When it was time for Gareth's obligatory afternoon rest, we found the bed to be too low for transferring from the chair to be easy. It was also surrounded by a metal frame and firmly attached to the wall on one side. I had to make sure no part of Gareth came into contact with the metal, especially when he would be staying in the same position for a long time. Because I couldn't get round to the far side of the bed, I had to stand precariously on the metal edge nearest to the wall whilst turning him in the middle of the night. During the daytime either Bethan or Matthew would help me lift him in and out of bed, thus alleviating some of these problems. In any case they were minor troubles in the scale of things, and the whole experience of the ferry was a success.

The Spanish motorways were empty and I could set the speed control of our automatic car and cruise along without using either foot. It was very hot outside, but the air-conditioning kept us cool. In fact I didn't find the driving stressful and my back and legs were rather better after the journey than before. This was the life! Spain was to be our holiday country for ever!

We had been booked into an allegedly accessible hotel halfway to our villa. When we found it, we were dismayed to see what looked like the whole town in and around it. It was a real struggle to get the chair up a long, steep and crowded ramp. The lift was only just big enough when Gareth's feet were crushed backwards and sideways. The rooms were quite astonishingly noisy and the dining room was down several steps, so quite out of Gareth's reach. Bethan and I set out from the hotel to find food. It was a dead, run-down area and absolutely nothing was open. We realised it was a fiesta day and everyone was enjoying themselves. With horror we saw a poster advertising a bullfight that very evening. Hastily we joined Matthew and Gareth. In determined mood the two youngsters revisited the bar and returned in triumph with tortillas and coffees. With this, plenty of chocolate and a game of cards, we celebrated our arrival in Spain. The night seemed very long as we listened to the rowdy revellers. It was also very stuffy, as naturally, the air-conditioning didn't work. The next morning we met for breakfast at the bar, now mercifully quiet, had more or less the same snack and then Gareth performed the dangerous feat of getting down the ramp. When we reached the van, he saw that the Chrysler badge on the front had been stolen. Apparently he had worried all night about what hundreds of festive Spaniards might have done to our unusual vehicle. We could always replace the badge . . .

Apart from this night the holiday was a great success. The house was clean and well equipped. There was a moment of panic when we saw the width of the door to the only suitable downstairs bedroom. Gareth had only a few millimetres on either side, but could just squeeze through – an interesting manoeuvre after a couple of glasses of red wine. So once again disaster was narrowly averted. We even found some places of historic interest with basic access for wheelchairs. (In our experience, provision is usually poor in Spain, and Italy not too good for that matter.)

With one accord we decided to return to Spain the following year. I found an accessible house further north than Catalonia so the journey was even easier. When we arrived, we found it to be next to a river which was overlooked by a shady balcony. Gareth could read there when it got hot. There was a big pool and a games room.

It was another really enjoyable holiday of which I have some fond memories together with one alarming one.

A particularly silly episode shows that not quite everything is laden with the burden of disability. Inevitably small creatures tend to feature in our experiences of hot countries, including spiders, beetles and lizards. This year the doors weren't particularly close fitting and, after one wet day, we were inundated with small frogs! These were very sweet and had to be saved from drying up, as they would away from water. To this end we kept a plastic cup, a square of cardboard and a soft brush at hand. I was the acknowledged expert in catching them and we sometimes laugh remembering an occasion when Matthew sensed movement under his bed, and it was in truth a large frog. I grabbed the equipment, making the immortal comment, 'It's a big one! Come on, little one.' Bethan and Matthew were convulsed with laughter and rendered incapable of helping. Gareth enjoyed the scene from his safe vantage point and I thought everyone had gone mad. The frog was persuaded into the cup with a disgusting soft plop and deposited outside before I was shown the idiocy of my remark.

Such an episode contrasts with another one. I was never very confident driving in Spain and our house was reached by an extraordinarily steep, narrow turning off a busy road. The roof of the corner house was actually level with the junction. The visibility was poor and I dreaded turning left which involved crossing the stream of traffic from a tricky hill-start. This was something we did regularly to get to the nearest shops and for Bethan to use the only public telephone to keep in touch with her partner. The owner of the corner house had erected a small white post on the right-hand side of the road to protect his roof from damage. Since our van was left-hand drive, I couldn't see this once I got to the steepest part of the hill. One day, after queuing here, I had completely forgotten about the post when starting my right turn, which should have been easy. Gareth shouted, 'Stop!' but I scraped the side of the van, drove a few yards and drew in to the side of the road as soon as possible. He was beside himself, because he thought that the sliding door, unluckily on that side of the van, wouldn't open and neither he nor the chair could get out. I was equally distraught and tearful as I was to blame. We exchanged some regrettable words before I had time to jump out and view the damage. There was a white line all along the side, but no dents and the door functioned perfectly. Shaken at this proof of how little it took to pierce our control of self and situation, we proceeded with our excursion.

The fortnight sped away and we returned to the coast determined to make Spain our holiday destination the following year, for the third time. We boarded with ease, but as we passed the information counter on the way to grabbing 'our' corner, heard an official say, 'Yes, a severe storm is forecast. Would you like some sea sickness tablets, one for children, two for adults?' Groups of passengers were standing around looking worried, all trying to find out exactly how bad the weather was likely to be, and we gathered that it was being taken very seriously by the crew. Apprehensively we stowed the luggage in our cabins and settled to a warm drink in case we were unable to eat later. Gradually the satisfaction of having finished driving in Spain, and the prospect of a lazy day before a comparatively short push for home, overcame the fears of a rough sea. We chatted and laughed as the ferry left the shelter of the port and started to pitch and roll. An hour later Matthew and I were feeling distinctly unwell and Gareth felt he should be lying down. Since he hasn't got the muscles necessary for being sick, we wondered what would happen when his digestive system made that command; an attack of diarrhoea we assumed, but didn't know. At three o'clock I didn't relish getting Gareth into bed in the stuffy, claustrophobic cabin with the noises of the engine and air-conditioning. Bethan looked after our corner while Matthew went to lie down. The sway of the sea made transferring dangerous, but we managed and Gareth stayed in that bed until lunchtime the next day. He felt queasy and couldn't face getting up. For the next twenty-four hours (the journey took an extra three and a half) we lay, listening for the terrifying crunching, grating noise as the ship suddenly and sickeningly dropped. It sounded just as if it had hit the bed of the ocean or a rock and would suddenly split in two. Rationally we told ourselves and each other that this couldn't be the case, but what we heard told us otherwise. There was no sense of night or day and, at one point when I thought it was impossible to bear it any longer, my watch told me there were fifteen more hours to go.

What could we do in an emergency? I could rush Gareth into his chair, but no one was going to make room for him in the panic to get to the lifeboats. Perhaps the children and I could drag him up or down the crowded stairs . . . Anyway I was soon past hypothetical worries as sickness and diarrhoea took over. It was best lying down, dozing, but I had to leap up frequently and lurch to the bathroom. I shall never forget turning Gareth every few hours, standing on the metal edge of the bed, trying to control bowels and stomach, whilst hoping he wouldn't be pitched to the floor. Any movement caused me waves of nausea, interspersed with a steady gnawing ache and feeling of dizziness and weakness.

From time to time our spirits were lifted by the sight of a pale face peering round the door. Bethan insisted she was feeling fine and was enjoying watching the spray covering the windows. Every so often she would see how Matthew was and report back to us. He, always a poor traveller, had been sick several times and was feeling dreadful. We had to pretend to be better than we were, and almost were so for a short while after her visit. Towards dawn, even she admitted to feelings of sickness and slept for a while. Without her messenger role, I suppose I would have forced myself to wander the corridors to see if they were alright. We were touched at being looked after, though this happened often when we were abroad, especially in anything involving linguistic capability.

The waves reduced in size as we approached Plymouth and we gathered shakily on deck with everything packed, longing for land. The only redeeming feature of sea-sickness is the speed of recovery. Within an hour or so of leaving the port, we were looking for somewhere to stop for a light meal. However we will never risk a long, or probably any, sea journey again. The events of those twenty seven hours entirely eclipsed the memories of the three pleasant ferry trips across the Bay of Biscay. Holiday choices narrowed further. It would be futile to look back to those carefree, pre-accident days for suggestions. Perhaps Eurotunnel was the only possibility . . .

8

Re-learning to live

Gareth was now used to breathing without support, was pushing himself around in his wheelchair, and his general health was steadily improving. However there had been no real change in his paralysis since the second he recognised its existence, just after the accident. We clung to the gradually-decreasing chance that he would begin to move again, despite the rehabilitation procedures which more or less assumed the opposite. Physiotherapists continued to work on teaching us to cope with the big, physical aspects of living with spinal injury, whilst simultaneously, occupational therapists aimed to make life as full and varied as possible. The latter began to fill in that awful vacuum we confronted when reluctantly considering what would happen if there never was any improvement.

As far as we remember, there was no set time for Gareth to have occupational therapy. We never knew when one of its practitioners, usually Gill who ran the department, would appear in the ward, often taking Gareth off to her centre. This was reached by a turning off the main corridor from ward six and included a large treatment room, a smaller one (part of which was set up as a kitchen and part devoted to more technologically advanced equipment), staff rooms and a laboratory where

Ian the technician worked. The latter had a special mixture of practical skills in handling different materials, ingenuity in fashioning these to solve the problems of specific patients, and enormous human sympathy. He wouldn't go home until he had finished, according to his high standards, the tasks he had set himself. The whole department was cheerful and friendly, and the staff painstaking in their efforts to widen the horizons of their disabled patients.

At this time the whole business of eating and drinking was a nightmare to Gareth. For one thing he never felt hungry and only forced himself to eat so that he would gain strength. But the main problem was that he couldn't manage the absolutely basic process of feeding himself – it was a cruel reversion to childhood. He had spent several weeks in bed, at one time being fed by a drip, then drinking using a 'bendy' straw and being spoon-fed solids. Here at Rookwood he could only sit in the wheelchair waiting for someone to feed him or hold a cup to his lips. None of us ever imagined that, if he stayed in his present condition, there would be ways of overcoming the problem. Not being the most patient person in the world, I dreaded the thought of every mealtime gobbling my own food and constantly watching to see whether Gareth had finished chewing his last mouthful.

In pre-accident days he had often been teased for his love of regular cups of tea and now, especially since copious drinking is very important to flush out the systems of paralysed patients, there were hot drinks mid-morning and afternoon, after meals and in the late evening. The only trouble was that the busy nurses had to hold these for all the people who couldn't do so themselves. Sometimes we had to listen to Gareth's account of how his tea had cooled and been thrown away untouched – 'And I was really looking forward to it!' he would complain. (This was ironic in a context where liquid intake and output had to be recorded in order to measure the extent of bladder retention; that cup would certainly have been included in the figures.) Soon the occupational therapy department got to work and there was a big improvement. First, Ian made him a lap tray with its base filled with polystyrene granules which would settle to ensure the whole thing was level, while the top was surrounded by a raised wooden edge and covered with a sticky-feeling, blue, plastic sheet to hold hot drinks and food steady. It was a good start, just to have food and drink on his own knees. Then there were experiments to see if Gareth could hold different sorts of mugs, all well-insulated (people with no feeling in their hands can easily get burnt), including two-handled ones. Then I was sitting with him one day when the afternoon tea was brought round. As usual I held the mug towards his mouth, only to be told nonchalantly, 'It's alright. I can do it myself!' Doubtfully I put it down on the tray and with intense delight watched Gareth slip the four rigid fingers of his right hand into the large handle, lift steadily and drink. 'I discovered this on my own this morning. It was annoying waiting and the nurses were busy so I thought I'd have a go.' We could hardly wait to show Bethan and Matthew when they came at the weekend. They were spellbound. It was an amazing breakthrough to useful action and it lifted our spirits for days. Gareth got so used to his independence in this that he got cross if all the wide-handled mugs had been used before the tea trolley got to him and he had to be helped.

Not many days later an occupational therapist brought Gareth a leather strap that fastened with velcro around his hand, just under the knuckles. On the underside there was a narrow pouch into which a spoon fitted so that it jutted out between the thumb and forefinger. He soon learnt to slide the strap on himself, tighten it using his teeth and manipulate food (as long as it was cut up) with ease. This seemed an absolutely brilliant invention – simple, relatively unobtrusive and providing the ability to perform such an important action independently. It cancelled at a stroke that tremendous loss of dignity in waiting, mouth open, for the next mouthful of food, especially if the feeder is in an obvious hurry, impatient to spoon in the next rapidly-cooling blob. Gareth would at least be spared this and it looked as if he would even be able to enjoy eating out with friends without feeling too conspicuous. In the worst eventuality of his remaining paralysed, at least he would be able to eat and drink more or less normally.

The next step in this long process of rehabilitation was thought to be Gareth learning to wash himself. One day when I arrived from school, an aggrieved husband gave me a spirited account of the pantomime he had been obliged to star in that morning. To begin with he had been woken early so that Gill could see how he could manage to perform his ablutions. He was lifted into a shower chair and pushed near a sink which was specially designed to be at an appropriate level, with space for the footrest underneath. Then a face cloth in the shape of a mitten was put on his right hand and soaped for him. He rubbed it over the parts of his body within reach and afterwards, sketchily, tried to rinse the same areas. It was still very difficult for him to sit upright without frequent tilting back, so not only did he get cold, but his blood pressure plummeted and he nearly fainted. Gareth thought this was a strange sort of independent action when it involved as much work for the occupational therapist or nurses as if they washed him themselves. 'I don't care about washing myself, now I'm like this', he grumbled. 'Why don't they just get me up as quickly as possible and stick me in front of a typewriter?'

This annoyance was not only conveyed to me, it seemed, and his reluctance to wash himself was reported at the next meeting of his 'team'. These teams were designated by different colours and each consisted of a ward nurse, a physiotherapist, an occupational therapist and possibly others. They would meet at least once a week in the hope of getting an all-round picture of the progress of their patients. Gareth used to suspect that, since everyone felt they should have something to report about each patient, there was a danger that the slightest incident could be blown up into some significance. In this instance he was categorised as someone who didn't want to help himself, preferring to rely on others, especially me. When he realised this, he was not only surprised but rather offended as well, since he thought he had only rationalised the situation. 'They think I'm a bone-idle idiot who's not even prepared to make an effort to get better. I ask you, why struggle to wash a strictly-limited area of myself when I'm shivering and half dead? I'll struggle to do most things, but this is plain stupid.' This was the second time Gareth suspected treatment of patients was rather stereotypical; those with his level of break were expected to follow roughly the same pattern of rehabilitation. As an academic he was desperate to make progress in writing, reading and computing – whatever else caused him severe discomfort he was happy to leave, at least until he was stronger.

However, when he was given an opportunity to shave himself, he was delighted. Gill brought to the ward a sheet of a white substance which could be cut, moulded and was self-adhesive when heated. She wrapped a rectangular piece around the shaver and used a flap to secure the base, thus forming a cylindrical holder. Then a handle was shaped around Gareth's fingers and pressed into position. It worked beautifully and, as it could be used when he was dry, warm and comfortable, was instantly adopted.

Proof that the criticism mentioned above was largely unfounded soon came to light in the large amount of time spent experimenting with ways to help Gareth resume his academic activities. Gill was exceptionally patient and full of initiative and nobody could criticise Gareth's motivation here. First of all he needed to write, and obviously couldn't do so by the normal method of gripping a pen between thumb and finger. Numerous contraptions were tried out. For instance, a rigid structure moulded to the shape of his hand and lower arm was attached by velcro and a pen fixed to it. This did work, but was cumbersome and eventually, Gareth discovered he could manage with a simple method found by Bethan. It involved weaving a pen between the three main fingers of the right hand and writing with the thumb upwards, and the nib next to the little finger. I still have his first attempt to sign his name after the accident – barely recognisable, but marking a breakthrough. Whenever he produced something that could just about be called writing, he was always filled with a sense of achievement, but also despaired at the enormous gulf between those results and what he had been able to do effortlessly since childhood.

At least equally important was to find some way of reading without having to get someone to turn each page for him. He tried out an automatic machine for this, but again it was very bulky and seemed to be more trouble than it was worth. For some time he used a kind of rubber thimble which would lightly stick to a page so its edge could be pushed towards the centre until it would turn over. Ultimately he didn't need this, using the side of a rigid finger to separate the pages. Matthew discovered a light, quite small, hinged bookstand which helped by keeping the book steady at a convenient angle.

By the time a few weeks at Rookwood had passed, Gareth knew he could manage to read by himself and that he could scrawl a word or two. But he needed to be able to use a computer if there was to be any chance of writing legibly and at length. Luckily, certain aspects of his work had come increasingly to require typewriting and then word-processing skills. Twenty years before the disaster we had both tried to teach ourselves to touch-type. Though hardly succeeding in this, we developed idiosyncratic styles, Gareth's in particular being fast and not too inaccurate. We proceeded through a series of typewriter correction techniques: fluid, strips and tapes. Finally we graduated to an Amstrad word processor, and at a stroke, solved all problems of correction. Now, before he could use this limited degree of computer literacy, he had to prove himself capable of operating keys – initially of an electric typewriter. His fingers, though rigid, did not have the power to depress these. After much patient trial and error on the part of the occupational therapy staff, another substantial, hard glove was devised with a rubber-tipped stick attached to the palm. He could direct the strength of his arm through the stick to a single key. At first this was very hit and miss, and always slow and inaccurate. Gareth kept saying, 'It's no good trying. I'll never be able to do any proper academic work again.' At weekends Matthew tried to counteract this perfectly justified pessimism: 'Of course you will, Dad. You've got a dictaphone and a secretary. Anyway we'll all write for you.' In any case, being able to type at all was an advance and Gareth persisted. For quite a long time he was allowed one of the few single rooms and the typewriter lived on a table at the foot of his bed. He managed to complete an external examiner's report and a book review, both promised before the accident. It was difficult to know whether to laugh or cry at the results, but Bethan corrected them on the Amstrad and saw they were posted. This was the strongest evidence to date that some kind of academic work would be possible, though its extent was highly questionable. I had set my heart on Gareth returning to work in Aberystwyth and it began to seem almost possible.

All the above examples of rehabilitation bear witness to the ingenuity and persistence of the occupational therapists. Though Gareth could only move his head, arms and hands in a limited way, he was now able to propel himself in a wheelchair, eat, drink, read, write and typewrite, all with some degree of independence. Unfortunately the things he was unable to do were infinitely more numerous and terribly depressing, but we could see some sort of existence emerging for a disabled Gareth, however unwelcome the latter concept remained. Yet we were still left with the central question of how anyone with such limited abilities and such major disabilities could support himself and a family.

We had part of the answer to this question when, quite soon after his admission to Rookwood, Gareth was visited by a cheerful, brightly-dressed lady whose job included providing information about social benefits for the disabled. She filled in the application forms for the disability allowance and explained its various components. This was very helpful as we were in complete ignorance of our rights in this area. What with this allowance, Gareth's occupational pension and whatever I could earn, it began to look as if we might just about survive financially. Naturally there would be a large drop in income and we agonised over what we would be able to afford to do, especially in relation to Bethan and Matthew. Precise calculation about income was impossible yet, but Gareth had a pretty clear idea of our usual expenses and the total seemed well beyond what we could hope for in our changed condition.

Over and above this basic question of survival hung the issue of whether we would ultimately get a financial settlement from the insurance company of the other driver. The quality of our future life depended on this. One of my first phone calls on the day after the accident had been to our much-respected family solicitor, and his firm had started to make enquiries immediately. Another aspect of this was due to the fact that I had seen details of the Spinal Injuries Association exhibited just inside the door of ward six. Gareth became a member as soon as possible, and what was so helpful to us at this time was the fact that they had a legal advisor who was expert in dealing with compensation claims. This lady, herself wheelchair-bound, came to see Gareth in Rookwood and from then on worked hand in glove with our family solicitor.

It was very encouraging for us all to see such an example of professional independence in someone who had been spinally injured. She pushed herself into the ward in her manually-operated chair with her briefcase on her lap. We learnt of various other cases she had been involved in and so found out how very complicated making a claim for compensation is. One thing was perfectly clear: if you don't know all the possible components of this, you lose out – no insurance company is going to tell you that you could have asked for more! After a long, invaluable session I walked back to the car with her and was astonished to see the way she got herself into the car, collapsed the chair and lifted it over the passenger seat and into the back. I wanted to help but was not allowed. She had a meticulous routine in which everything was positioned in reach – and this was fool-proof, unless, for example, some idiot ignored the polite request on the window not to park too near.

We soon found out how lengthy the whole claims process is. One of the starting points was an assessment of Gareth's condition by the Rookwood consultant. We were told there was nothing to do but wait while he ploughed through a pile of similar exercises, each one time-consuming. A couple of weeks passed without result and there was no proper procedure for hurrying someone in such an elevated position. In the end I believe some kind soul, sensing Gareth's distress, secretly moved his form near to the top of the pile! We were soon summoned to the consultant's office to hear his prediction of Gareth's ultimate condition and hence an outline of his future needs. I had been worrying about what we might hear and its effect on him. In this I was right. There was no mention made of the slightest chance of recovery – his paralysis was irreversible. In fairness to the consultant, he made it clear that he had to say this or the claim couldn't go ahead. It was depressing though and I wondered if we could cope with what we were to hear when the section on life-expectancy was reached. Suppose he said Gareth would in all probability live two years, or five, or even ten? I sat in utter misery on the edge of my chair, but the consultant kindly told us he had estimated Gareth's life-expectancy to be as near to the normal for men as he convincingly could, just three years less in fact. We relaxed again and at last realised that he was doing his level best to gain the best compensation he could for us.

Our family solicitor, with advice from the Spinal Injuries legal advisor, worked on the details of the claim. The final compensation figure offered was given as a single figure, but there was nothing random about it. Calculations were made about what it would cost yearly for Gareth to live more or less as before, in terms of, for example, housing, car, clothes and holidays. Specialised equipment and adaptation to the home were, of course, included in the total. Expert advice was needed in each aspect of these claims. Throughout, great care was exercised to ensure that his previous standard of living would not be exceeded. A 'multiplier' was applied to the annual total. Oddly enough this was not, as I expected, simply the number of years Gareth could expect to live, but the result of the application of a set formula which took into account, amongst other things, the amount of interest that would be gained on a specific, decreasing sum of money. I was alarmed at the gap between the multiplier and life-expectancy – what would we do if Gareth lived beyond the former figure or hopefully even the latter? If we did have a settlement, we would have to be careful not to approach the estimated yearly expenditure or we might face serious financial difficulties in our last days.

We were very relieved that the other driver's well-known insurance company had accepted liability to pay compensation, so our advisors assured us that there would be a settlement, but obviously that the amount would have to be negotiated. We knew that the claim had to be lodged with the court within three years of the accident, but that this could well be the start of lengthy disputes. As it turned out, the insurance company eventually decided it was cheaper to settle the claim fairly quickly out of court. About three years from the accident we knew our financial position and could feel more secure about the future. At least we would have money for a good wheelchair, adapted vehicle and alterations to the house. By no means all spinally-injured people are as fortunate in this respect.

The most significant source of information about a possible way of life for post-accident Gareth was the plethora of paralysed people with whom he lived. For this he only needed to look around and exchange casual gossip. Some were in the early stages of rehabilitation, but many had been readmitted owing to a particular problem that had arisen at home. It was easy to learn something of the pre-accident life and see all too clearly the struggles to retain something of this. For instance, one young man was readmitted with pressure sores after sitting on a pavement for five hours at a pop festival. He was in hospital for five months; as a nurse put it, 'one month for every hour you enjoyed yourself.' I suppose that the next time he would sadly stay in his wheelchair, resisting the temptation to be once again one of the boys. Another man who retained the use of his upper body and hands after a car crash was fiercely protective of his independence, refusing all nursing support and trying to live as before. He used mirrors to check for pressure sores and, when one developed, tried to heal it himself. The result was plastic surgery and months in Rookwood. What both cases told us is that disabled people ignore their new physical limitations at their peril. The first young man hoped his skin could cope with extra pressure from sitting on concrete – just the once. The other hoped that common sense could identify a pressure sore and go on to cure it. Already we had been told by many nurses never, ever, to forget skin sensitivity. It looked as if some people did that and suffered horribly as a result. Perhaps there were many examples out in the world of disabled people who managed this problem successfully, but with lack of evidence, we found Gareth's future very disquieting. What price a carefree life now?

Arguably, the saddest cases of all were those injured in sporting accidents. The victims were usually young, and whether professional or amateur, tended to have been at the peak of physical condition at the time of the accident. The difference for them between their condition before and after the accident was inevitably so enormous that, not only would it be almost impossible to accept being unable to move, but also any sort of return to the main features of a former life would be almost certainly ruled out. One fellow patient had crushed a few vertebrae in a freak diving accident. Following another diver into a deep, public pool, currents unaccountably pulled him forcefully to the floor. He had an office job and lived with a partner and their toddler. They were so young, with everything before them. Sometimes he would turn up pop music on his radio very loud, afterwards apologising to Gareth saying, 'I want to drown everything out, to forget.' Another fit young man fell off his surfboard in the shallows, hitting his head on the sand and breaking his neck. Again his life would be appallingly different thereafter.

From time to time we hear in the news that a rugby player has damaged his neck. Gwyn Jones, the former Welsh captain, is a relatively recent example. Luckily, he has made a remarkable recovery and can walk again – and has a career in the media and medicine. Gareth got to know one player who was not as fortunate. He had a very high break and could not move his hands or arms, propelling his wheelchair by varying the air pressure to a tube in his mouth. Virtually all of his body was paralysed, though he could breathe unaided, and speak. In spite of the degree of frustration he must have experienced he was usually bright and talkative. He had three young children whom his wife brought in regularly to see their father. It is hard to think about what it meant to that sportsman not to be able to run about in the garden with his children. His wife was wonderful and, apparently, some of the extended family who lived locally were very supportive. Yet his life had changed almost beyond recognition.

Gareth saw that the more physically active pre-accident life was, the greater the change after paralysis. Luckily for him, much as he had always enjoyed sport, it was by no means the most important element of his life. Yet there was an enormous vacuum created when the chance of the occasional game of tennis or squash was removed. He continued his sadly realistic observation of his fellow patients – what did disabled people do for pleasure, when possibly all and certainly most of their established pastimes had been ruled out? There was usually loud pop music in the ward and television for sport and 'soaps'. It was the convention to sneer at hospital food and many patients, especially the younger ones, enjoyed sending out for takeaways. Gareth never did this, finding the food provided adequate and not feeling hungry anyway. (His visitors kept him well stocked with fruit and chocolate but he was equally unable to eat much of these.) Yet for some people it seemed a slight escape from hospital to eat food from the outside. The real treat, however, was to go down the pub.

Occasionally some of the nurses would give up an evening at weekends to wheel patients down a steep hill to the local, which was sympathetic to wheelchair customers. Gareth, never having been one to spend much time in pubs, was, in his present state, decidedly against joining in. However, at last, touched by the kindness of the nurses coming back to Rookwood dressed smartly in civvies, he responded to their persuasion. We joined a convoy of six or eight wheelchairs leaving the ward, everyone in high spirits. It was quite a struggle to stop Gareth disappearing down the hill in a runaway chair. Equally difficult was getting up and down the kerbs at the bottom, and crossing the road was a nightmare. Somehow, when eventually gathered at the bar, the group of wheelchairs seemed discouragingly incongruous, their occupants far removed from the other normal, healthy people sitting around. Not that there was a lack of kind smiles and salutations – far from it – and the nurses did their best to be sociable, but for Gareth at least, the consciousness of his disability was heightened. He tried to drink half a pint of lager and be sociable, but I could see what misery the whole situation was for him. He was glad to set off for Rookwood quite soon, using the excuse of my late return to Pennard. Getting up the hill was exhausting and I was very glad to get him back safely. He was pleased to have shown his willingness to join in and that he appreciated the efforts of the nurses, but he never went again. The outing planned to give entertainment to the patients had shown Gareth that in all probability he could never again pass as one of the crowd. He would be different, noticeable, even subject to patronising kindness. How was he to bear this?

Sometimes, if they had suitable transport, visitors were allowed to take patients out for a drink. Occasionally they came back the worse for wear. A combination of medical drugs and changed body state sometimes enhanced the effect of alcohol, so that an amount that would have been innocuous in earlier days could be quite dangerous. I remember someone being rushed in, wrapped in foil and smothered in duvets, since his temperature had dropped alarmingly after a couple of pints. The visitors were very sheepish, saying he had been acting out of bravado and could not be stopped. The nurses were good-humoured, understanding precisely what had made him act like that – he wanted to be like the other drinkers, able to 'knock it back'. As Gareth had felt, he didn't want to be different.

Many patients boasted of going to the pub when at home, too. In some cases it seemed the only expedition they made with any degree of regularity and had become the *raison d'etre* of their lives. Even with specialised transport, journeys can be a problem for disabled people, and a 'local' becomes a comparatively easy source of conviviality. Most of the spinally-injured patients we got to know had been obliged to give up work, but did it inevitably follow that life was to be no more than lazing around, eating, watching television, listening to music and visiting one's local? We all knew and were frightened by the knowledge that Gareth, much as he enjoyed these things, needed more. But would his ability to read unaided and his slight computer skills be enough to form the basis of a life he could find satisfying? It was deeply worrying.

Almost all the inmates of Rookwood were obsessed with going home, as if once there everything would be alright again. But clearly this couldn't be a magical, happy ending to a nightmare situation. The things that people did at Rookwood must be pretty accurate pointers to what they could do at home, albeit in happier surroundings. One example underlined this point for us. A fellow patient whom we came to like and respect was discharged from hospital full of plans for how he would organise his house and continue his hobbies. When he was readmitted some weeks later for a routine check, we were saddened to see the change in his personality. His optimism and resilience seemed to have been defeated by the realities of paralysed existence. There was a new, quiet reserve and no mention of any plans. This was a remarkable and brave man, and I sincerely hope we were completely wrong in our judgement of how he coped at home.

In spite of such warnings, Gareth began to get desperate in his need to be at home. For a long time at Rookwood he had seen progress, not in terms of his main objective, overcoming paralysis, but in terms of increased strength and in learning ways to use his remaining movement to the best advantage. Now he felt he had reached a plateau and could continue the struggle at home, free from the horrors of institutional living. I had spent the greater part of virtually every day at Rookwood and had learnt many things about how to care for him. Oddly enough I hadn't thought out the details of what I would be required to do when he did come home or panicked about the responsibility. I just wanted him to be with the family and tried to feel confident that, sooner or later, I would help make it possible for him to move again. Beneath the surface of life during these months that I have described in fairly neutral terms lay the pure desperation of Gareth's condition and the gradual weakening of the hope for a complete cure. Yet I was determined we would keep that hope alive. In the meantime we would do everything for the rehabilitation that one day, we sometimes almost believed, would not be necessary.

Interlude

The same and not the same

An early visitor to Cardiff Royal Infirmary had come to cheer his close friend and colleague who was lying paralysed and barely conscious in Intensive Care. He was denied admittance, so turned his attention to comforting the patient's wife and daughter. Rather than give voice to the crushing emotion they all felt, he asked for a message to be passed on – one that implicitly asserted that nothing had fundamentally changed – 'Tell him I've taken his name in vain and agreed we'll edit another volume for our Welsh history series.' The two women smiled drearily at each other; such a request seemed at the time to be infinitely removed from the agonising questions of survival and recovery. Yet on reflection it revealed a clear understanding of the injured man's nature and, equally clearly, was designed to deflect their minds from those very questions which haunted them day and night.

Many other friends and colleagues who flocked to see Gareth carried on discussion of professional commitments when they were allowed into Intensive Care, and later, other wards. He was fully in charge of a university department on the day of the accident and remained nominally in post. Luckily the summer term was over, and the students had gone home, though they were to return the following week for their degree ceremony.

Gareth's administrative officer brought any vitally important mail to the hospital from time to time. Obviously there was little he could do in his perilous state, but it was very good for his morale that he should be kept informed. Two years previously he had been in the unique position of being a member of both the National Curriculum Working Group for History and the National History Committee for Wales. Partly because of this he was involved in a project, based in Aberystwyth, on the provision of standard tests at Key Stage 3 (14-year-old pupils) in history. The people involved were absolutely determined that Gareth should continue to work with them, visiting CRI regularly, and eventually, actually held two committee meetings in the day room at Rookwood! He was also, at the time of the accident, chairman of the working party relating to the setting up of a Curriculum Cymreig – that is, a special syllabus for schools in Wales. Drafts of the documents were brought to Gareth for comment. With great kindness the members of this working party ensured Gareth's name appeared as chairman on the resulting working paper, though he felt this was hardly merited!

Such examples show not only how Gareth's contribution to all sorts of educational matters was appreciated, but also gives some idea of the extent to which other people realised that work was of crucial importance to him – and so aimed for his continued involvement. I certainly shared this view and, for ages, was determined that somehow or another Gareth would return to what he found so rewarding, that his career as far as possible would be uninterrupted by the disaster. He was less sure and it gradually became apparent during the period from December when he returned home, to the following summer when he would need to make a decision, that it wasn't feasible. His health was still in a precarious state and any improvement in it either non-existent or imperceptible. It took an least an hour to get him up and dressed; he needed a rest in the afternoon and couldn't handle papers very easily or write more than a few words by hand. Old College was, as the name suggests, a far from modern building. Some of the ground floor was accessible and a room could have been turned into his office, but most of it was completely unsuitable. He needed to attend meetings in all sorts of buildings, not only in Aberystwyth, but in many other areas of Wales and England, the majority of which he might never be able to enter. I was prepared to give up work and become a kind of secretary-cum-nurse, but Gareth was adamant that if he couldn't do the job properly, he wasn't going to do it at all. The officials at the University had been particularly kind, keeping his post open by appointing an acting head of department for a whole academic year (though several of them have since admitted they thought all along that the likelihood of Gareth's return was very remote).

So the man who had planned to retire at sixty three was, ten years too early, unemployed. It is impossible to describe adequately the blow this was to him. Many colleagues were eager to help establish some continuity between his life before and after the accident. To an extent this has been achieved. Ten years later Gareth, first as Research Professor, now Emeritus Professor, still has professional engagements. Indeed at no time did he quite give up. He gives lectures to many different audiences, including university students and staff, conferences and historical societies. So in this respect, there is some continuity – it is the same and not the same.

In the old days, giving lectures was an ordinary, almost routine, part of the job – some requiring more preparation than others. The actual content of the lecture was then the only concern and Gareth would speak from brief notes or headings. Getting to the venue would be no more than a train or car journey and the process of entering the building would probably go unnoticed. These days the content is as important as ever, though now Gareth needs the reassurance of having the whole text typed out carefully. He will speak for five or ten minutes without any notes, but for longer lectures he has the complete script. This is always immaculately prepared quite some time in advance of the occasion. However, this is only one of many things to consider when planning the visit.

We start the physical preparations the day before with such humdrum matters as hair-washing (unless by good luck this happens to coincide with Gareth's weekly shower). This involves placing a bowl on the kitchen floor near the sink and a special close-fitting tray placed round his neck, so that the water running off the head is channelled into the bowl. It is quite difficult to get the back of the chair at the right angle so that the water doesn't trickle down his neck instead of draining away. I try to shampoo and rinse quickly, since his position is decidedly uncomfortable, and in spite of waterproof sheets and towels, the odd bit of shirt will get damp. Next we move into the main room for hair-drying and combing, which is the pleasant part of the experience. He loves the feeling of his wet head being roughly massaged – one of the true sensations he has left.

The next morning, special care is given to continence procedures and comparatively tidy clothes are put on. Gareth finds the conventional jackets he always wore too restricting, so the only element of choice is deciding which matching shirt and sweater to wear. His skin can only tolerate shiny, uncreasable, tracksuit bottoms, so these have to be worn on every occasion. (I have tried time and again to get hold of that kind of material so I could make some more formal trousers for him, but have failed.) When dressed and breakfasted we proceed to the back door where I check Gareth over for the last time, re-comb his hair, empty the leg bag and tuck his jumper down the back and sides of the chair, even though it will immediately ride up again. Next we go through the contents of the black bag which fits on the back of the chair: lecture, lap-tray, and insulated cup and spoon with its special holder. Finally I collect my coat and handbag, then put on Gareth's 'Darth Vader' woollen cape (which I made since nothing suitable seemed to exist). The short journey to the van is a nightmare on very cold or wet days – and nights are infinitely worse. In these instances I prop the side gate open and operate the sliding door and ramp, before shouting to Gareth, who puts the chair on to fast speed and dashes through the door (one centimetre clearance each side), along the path and into the van. Unfortunately he has to pause on the ramp to raise the footplate to stop it grounding, but not high enough to bump his head on the top of the door surround. While I lock up the house, he performs the very difficult manoeuvre of getting the chair into the automatic tie-down, with absolutely no spare space on either side. This often takes a few attempts and leaves Gareth annoyed with himself and the design. I put on his headrest and fasten the safety belt which he reaches down to me.

After all this performance the actual business of driving seems restful, unless we have a long or difficult journey. Gareth will have worked it all out days ago and gives me precise directions. He will also have checked that the venue is accessible and found out where to park. Sometimes we have to be met and taken through, for instance, a side gate, or directed to a special disabled parking area. Often we can't enter a building through the usual entrance and have to be taken to wherever there is level access. Sometimes we have to use our own ramp which has to be taken to and from the car; occasionally one is provided. In any case it is always a relief to reach the lecture room, especially if we haven't been able to see for ourselves in advance that access really is possible.

I will have punched a hole through the top corner of the pages of the lecture and fastened them with the shortest 'treasury' tag, which allows just the right degree of flexibility for page turning. Before he starts, I turn up the bottom right-hand corner of each page so Gareth can manipulate them with his unyielding hands. He raises his chair to its highest position and places the folder on his tray which rests on his knees. (It's often impossible for him to get on any platform and lecterns are obviously unsuitable because there is nowhere for his feet to go.) There's usually a glass of water available, but almost certainly out of his reach and it's too risky to have it on the tray with the lecture – even a small spasm would create mayhem. In the early days he used to have a clip-on microphone because his voice was so weak, but manages without one now except in very big rooms. For more important lectures I sit as near the front as possible, ready to dash forward with a sip of water or to turn an errant page, though I've never been obliged to do this. Sometimes I hang around in the building where I could be quickly found. Nowadays, since we have a mobile telephone, I can even do some local shopping, depending on the circumstances of the lecture.

At last Gareth can draw breath and begin his lecture. In advance he is confident about its delivery, less so of being stopped by an awkward page-turn. But now he forgets all the practical problems, concentrates on the task in hand and always succeeds admirably. He sits relaxed in his wheelchair, looking normal and behaving as an academic should. The audience think, 'Isn't he wonderful, carrying on just the same as before.' No concessions are needed – this is our aim. There is no sign of any extra preparation or any hint of possible disaster. For that hour or two he essentially is the same, though we know with dismal certainty that in so many ways he really is not and never will be.

Gareth's major books have tended to be based to a large extent on primary sources. Often he would need to find and analyse these in places such as the British Museum or the Public Record Office. Until the accident the problem was always how to find sufficient time for this, the part of his job he enjoyed above all. Since he became paralysed, even browsing through books in a library is impossible without assistance, though the quality of the help he receives from the staff of the University Education library is magnificent and far beyond the call of duty. Indeed he's not prepared to go much further afield, feeling that the frustrations would far outweigh any advantages. Anyway, how many libraries have sufficient space between shelves? Gareth has decided reluctantly that the rest of his writings will be based on secondary sources which can be brought to the house. To my great sadness he cancelled a contract he had with Macmillan for a book which would have involved much research of a kind he feels would be impossible in his present state. How much more sad he must have been as he typed the letter.

Yet he hasn't given up writing, having for instance, published a book of his essays, called *The Education of a Nation*, in 1997. He also co-edited with Dai Smith a millennium history of Wales, entitled *The People of Wales* in 1999. Apart from writing numerous articles and chapters in books, he has also edited twelve numbers of *The Welsh Journal of Education*. So in this respect too he is active as an academic, but not quite in the way he thought. Once again he finds himself to be the same and not the same. Two years ago he was delighted to find his work, pre- and post-accident, bracketed together in the award of a D.Litt. – a research degree of distinction.

How can Gareth, who at Rookwood could only painstakingly press one key of a typewriter at a time using a rod attached to a rigid glove, achieve all this? He continued to use this method at home with his Amstrad computer for quite some time. The big breakthrough came when one of my brothers-in-law found out all there was to know about voice-operated computers and, eventually, spent a couple of weekends installing the best possible system here and training Gareth how to use it.

Gareth was able to progress from single key typing to miraculously having his spoken words turned into printed ones. It is by no means one hundred per cent accurate and there is always some correction to be done, even using the more advanced system that the same relation installed four years later. Yet the improvement in what it is possible for Gareth to achieve is dramatic. Without help of any sort he can write, edit and print out his work. The most I do is to ensure there is paper in the printer and perhaps file or post the results. As an editor he can now ask for his material on disk (or even scan the printed page into his computer), make corrections on the screen and then print a final version. He can also access libraries on the internet, again helping his research. Finally he can send and receive fax or e-mail messages completely unaided.

As with the delivery of lectures and the kind of research undertaken, there are highly significant changes in the way this research can be carried on, though a basic continuity remains. Gareth will never be able to write freely or to pull down a selected book from a shelf, yet he still can produce important work. He can't do as much nor work as quickly, partly because he only feels well enough to work in the morning, yet there has been a technologically-aided liberation for which he is very thankful.

Gareth has always loved the social side of his job. He would meet not only staff and students in his department and the rest of the university, but would foster links with the community and with schools. He got on well with people and seemed popular wherever he went. No retirement activities could quite replace that day-by-day constant contact with so many others. Yet he does go to

Llandaff and ransacked the local shops for more interesting additions. After lunch on Sunday we strolled (can you stroll in a wheelchair?) about the grounds together, returning with something of a feeling of homecoming. It was the nearest we had got to family living for months on end.

I was absolutely determined to prove we could cope on our own, so that Dr Grove would have the confidence to discharge Gareth very soon. A nurse from ward six came on Saturday morning to check all was well and give me guidance in getting him up – after all, this was the very first time I'd been entrusted with such a thing. The second morning she just did the medical tasks and left me to do the washing and dressing. This took a long time and I expended a lot of energy in moving his static body, though he was very thin. Finally I had to transfer Gareth from bed to chair using a ceiling hoist. I was very nervous, though I had been shown how to position the sling under him, attach it to the mechanism, and push buttons on a hand control for lift-off and sideways movement. Until this morning I'd hardly moved a paralysed Gareth about at all. As I tilted him to one side to get the sling under, it looked as if he would tip out over the wheelchair arm. Luckily he didn't. Soon I was glad to be sitting at the table with Gareth and Matthew peacefully eating our cornflakes, safe in the knowledge that I had a few hours respite before the next transfer from chair to bed.

There were no health scares over the weekend to our delight, and only two slight panics. Once I exclaimed in terror, 'Oh no! You should have had your tablets half an hour ago!' I thought that it could be of vital importance to have them absolutely regularly and watched Gareth nervously for a few hours. It didn't seem to have made any difference and I never owned up – for fear I would be judged too scatterbrained to look after him. Once too I had to sneak back to the ward for a sterile dressing pack used to clean the 'trache' hole. They were in the drawer at the side of Gareth's bed and, to my relief, no one took any notice of me. All in all, considering he was still in a rather unstable condition, requiring fairly frequent doses of ephedrine and tilting back in the chair, I was pleased. I hadn't needed to send for a nurse, though Dr Grove was certainly right – it was very reassuring to know they were a stone's throw away.

A different challenge I had to face was waking at two and five o'clock to change Gareth's position, and then at eight to start getting up. We were all exhausted after the strain of the last months and I tended to sleep heavily whenever I had a chance. Would I sleep through the alarm? Would Gareth as a result get bedsores and have to stay yet longer in hospital? In spite of these very real worries, I leapt up instantly each time and almost immediately fell back to sleep afterwards. In the morning I was feeling so pleased with myself that I forgot to be tired.

Gareth revelled in the lack of constant intrusion, after months of living in a ward of other people with little space between the beds, and strangers dealing with the most intimate bodily functions. Although very sociable he had always been an intensely private person. The invasion of this privacy was a bitter aspect of his changed condition. Naturally it was quite different having me doing things he shrank from when performed by nurses, however expert and kindly. The whole weekend was a tremendous uplift out of the gloom which, though sometimes not fully recognised in its permanence, overshadowed every aspect of our lives.

Sunday night came and a reluctant Gareth was returned to ward six before Matthew and I set off for Swansea. It was hard leaving him looking so sad. Having tasted freedom and a near independence of hospital, he felt the restrictions of communal life more than ever. He was always depressed when I left and, in these days before we had a mobile phone, worried that I would have an accident or break down on the way home. This evening would be infinitely worse than usual as he looked anew at the familiar setting of ward six. Luckily for me, I didn't see him settle into resignation and submission to his fate while he waited to be put to bed – but I imagined the scene as I drove. In her ward round next morning Dr Grove told him that an ambulance had been arranged to take him home the following weekend, so once again there was something to raise his spirits. When I arrived the next afternoon, wondering how he would be, I was met very cheerfully and heard the glad news.

Ever since the chances of Gareth remaining paralysed grew more substantial, we had given thought to whether we could adapt our home to suit his needs or whether we would have to add to the disruption of our lives by moving. Fortunately we lived in a dormer bungalow with four rooms downstairs, including a large through-lounge. Two of these rooms had been called bedrooms in the original specification of the house. However, we used one as a study and the other doubled as spare bedroom and music room. At first there were only two bedrooms upstairs, but as Bethan and Matthew grew too old to share, we added a two-room extension. This meant the functions of the downstairs rooms had stayed fixed, but now, in discussion with a builder, we saw they could be reorganised. (We considered and discounted the possibility of building a lift to get Gareth upstairs.) The present study could become a bedroom, with an *en suite* shower room made from the adjoining small cloakroom. The music equipment, except for the very heavy piano, could go upstairs, as would a convertible settee and chests of drawers, and that room would become his study. Upstairs we would dismantle the snooker table which more or less filled the biggest of the rooms and use the space for computers, musical instruments, stands, books and the displaced furniture. He would possibly never see the upstairs again, but the whole of the ground floor was completely flat, so there would be access to through-lounge, kitchen, study and bedroom, though the turning circle into the study was tight. Anyway, it would have to do: the expense of a move seemed beyond us, let alone the organisation and stress.

At the time of Gareth's first weekend home after the accident there was nothing except a sketch to show for our plans. One of the things we had to decide in advance was where he could sleep until we sorted things out. The existing study had to be emptied ready for the builders, so that left the music room. We disposed of the double bed kept until then for visitors and carried everything else upstairs as planned. There was nothing but the piano left and, had we been able to leave it at that, there would have been plenty of space for the single bed Gareth would use this weekend. In fact we had to give priority to emptying the old study, and an old friend willingly helped. He unscrewed bookcases from the walls, and carried in the enormous desk on which Gareth kept his computer and where he always worked. It fitted nicely under the window. Also, he started to move bookcases, having to clear them of books before they could be lifted. It was heavy work which Matthew and I completed late in the evenings when I got back from the hospital. It was also slow going. The volume of books and papers was amazing, and disordered piles covered most of the floor space. Somehow the bed was in position and there was just about enough space to squeeze around it when Saturday morning arrived. The chaos didn't disturb us, since we knew it would only be temporary.

Bethan came home from Bristol and she, Matthew and I eagerly awaited the arrival of the ambulance. It was later than we hoped because, though we didn't know it at the time, the driver was worried about insurance cover for a wheelchair passenger when there was no safe anchorage. Luckily he was persuaded it would be alright. It was now early November and Gareth had last left home on 29 June. Coming home had been an impossible dream for what seemed an eternity. Dr Grove, with her usual psychological insight, had warned him that, when it actually happened, coming home could be the saddest experience of all. We'd already seen disillusionment about this in some fellow patients when they came back to hospital after being at home. Usually people are only allowed to leave hospital when they are cured and so the irrational feeling is, 'Now everything will be alright again.' In the case of spinal injury, it is not. It is one thing to walk through the door and drive off to work; quite another to be carried in and dumped helpless in a corner.

So many of the ordinary little activities that were carried on automatically, and were the building blocks of life, were now probably beyond a tetraplegic forever – and the realisation of this can be a terrible blow. We had talked about this and hoped we could somehow rise above such negative feelings; but were terrified that the one thing that had kept Gareth sane through all his despair should fail him.

At length we three heard the ambulance drive up and rushed out in a body. There were no ramps up to the back or front door at this stage, but the men carried Gareth in with ease. He had a rapturous welcome and soon we were drinking a celebratory cup of tea in a welter of excited chatter. It was odd to see him in a wheelchair instead of his favourite armchair, but he looked round at the room he had so often visualised as he lay in Rookwood and soaked in the delight of being utterly and completely at home. Our exuberance created unlimited optimism and we all felt quite sure he would get better now. The family would see to it. All too soon it was time to give his skin a break from continuous pressure, so Bethan and Matthew lifted him bodily from the chair in the hall and carried him on to the bed. (There was no space for the chair in that cluttered room.) He lay there for an hour, smiling beatifically, far too happy to sleep. While he rested, I seized the opportunity of cooking lunch and, once he was upright again, we had a family meal, gloating at being all four together at home once more. There was no dwelling on Dr Grove's forebodings – not for Gareth, not for any of us.

It was the Saturday nearest to bonfire night and we were not going to miss out on our customary celebrations.

Matthew and I had chosen fireworks in Llandaff and there was enough wood in the garden to build a bonfire big enough to bake potatoes, cook sausages, and toast marshmallows. Though it was mild and dry, Gareth stayed inside rather than tempt providence on his first return home. He sat by the window of the through-lounge and we took it in turns to keep him company, whilst the rest cooked, or lit fireworks. I am sure the thought was in each of our minds that previously it had always been Gareth's job to do the latter, but no one mentioned it and in our thankfulness it seemed the slightest of shadows. From time to time we opened the window and posted in the tiniest of baked potatoes and burnt sausages. Then there was the hilarity of my easing a brown-capped marshmallow, molten and hot inside, into Gareth's open mouth. The fireworks, though as ever not a huge, expensive selection, seemed to symbolise our leaping spirits. As we gathered indoors at the end, smelling of wood smoke, Gareth said, 'Life may be worth living after all!'

There were some worries relating to his present physical condition underlying these glad celebrations, and these rose to the surface as night approached. The 'trache' hole in his throat still gaped open, and going with this was the possibility of infection. The real problem was the indwelling catheter which could block and cause the dreaded, dangerous autonomic dysreflexia. Once I had prepared Gareth for sleeping and settled in my sleeping bag on a put-u-up in the hall, I started to worry. Urgent action would be needed. I didn't know how to remove the catheter, and the nearest hospital was seven miles away. Sometimes there seemed to be long spaces between bladder activity and I started to panic. If there was a blockage, it was either a case of dressing Gareth and somehow getting him into my Metro, or calling an ambulance. We might get to the hospital too late! As it happened the night passed uneventfully, except for the routine changing of his position every few hours.

Until the evening before Gareth came home, I had assumed I would take sole responsibility for his care. At about ten o'clock the phone rang and an oriental-accented voice announced its owner to be the chief local district nurse. I outlined some of my worries and her response was, 'I will do it all. Everything will be alright. I will come every morning.' She was so friendly and encouraging that most of my fears melted away. This service must have been arranged through our GP, though no one thought to tell Gareth or me. I wish that particular communication gap had been filled as it would have saved me considerable fears about my competence to perform the strictly medical side of his care.

Having survived Saturday night, we waited anxiously the next morning for the nurse. This energetic lady arrived at about nine o'clock and, in a wonderfully reassuring torrent of words, outlined all the help she would organise whenever Gareth was at home. One of her team would give all the necessary medical treatment, then wash and dress him each morning. Others could get him in and out of bed in the afternoon and turn him at night. I was so relieved, feeling that my efforts would be monitored by experts and he would be very much safer. There would even be a case conference at Rookwood which she would attend where she would speak to each member of his team to get full information about his condition and needs.

Once Gareth was up and breakfasted, he read the Sunday papers in a leisurely manner. We found that the wheelchair fitted perfectly under our circular table, which had a lever so that it could be raised or lowered. For the first time since the accident he could spread a newspaper in front of him and turn pages with something approaching comfort. We all enjoyed our conventional Sunday lunch, again relishing being a complete family, but also trying to suppress the thought that the arrival of the ambulance was growing nearer. I was sad not to be able to see him settling back into Rookwood, but it would have been silly for me to follow the ambulance there, only to drive home more or less straight away. It was a dreadful moment when he actually left home and it must have been even worse when he re-entered the ward. Yet the weekend had to be considered a brilliant success: we had proved conclusively that it was safe for Gareth to come home. No one dwelt on the restricted life he would have to lead – we only wanted him to be at home.

After this weekend, hospital conditions became more and more irksome to him. They hadn't changed; he had. Now that he knew he could be cared for at home, he strongly resented being looked after by strangers and being surrounded by other patients day and night. It was by now all too clear to him that there was no new method to try to combat his paralysis. Visits to the physiotherapy room and the gym became rather stereotyped, and the occupational therapists had done all they could. The days dragged along in a succession of what had begun to seem meaningless activities. Yet in some ways he could be considered far more fortunate than many others in his position. At least I was able to be with him at least seven hours a day; longer at weekends with Matthew and sometimes Bethan. His supply of visitors never dried up. Several Cardiff, Swansea and Aberystwyth friends appeared remarkably regularly, but many, many people came at irregular intervals. My sisters continued to be wonderfully supportive, in person when possible, otherwise by post and telephone. Each day the mail brought cards and letters from other friends. To begin with we kept his little area festooned with scores of these, then saw it was tactless when some people had so very few. From then on a small selection reminded Gareth of his well-wishers. Yet, in spite of all this continued and much appreciated evidence of concern and affection, the basic, totally unresolved problem of paralysis couldn't fail to produce despair – and home seemed the only place that could nurture hope.

We were only allowed ambulance transport every fourth weekend, but rather than wait so long, we took advantage of a kind offer from a neighbour who had a Dormobile. It was difficult to get the wheelchair in through the side entrance of her van, but we managed in the end and Gareth had a longer time at home, from Friday to Sunday evenings. By the following weekend we determined to be independent, so as to be secure in the knowledge that the lack of transport was not ever going to hinder escape. Ian made us a rather longer sliding board for transferring Gareth into the front passenger seat of my Metro. One of the physiotherapists came out to the car park to show me how to do it. I always felt this was very dangerous when I did it, likely to end with Gareth bruised at best, and at worst on the floor. However, nothing would deter him; he was absolute in his determination to get home.

Late that Friday afternoon I eventually managed to wedge him into the Metro. He was in a not-very-comfortable position and felt unwell. He insisted on starting out, but on the motorway his vision began to break up and he was almost fainting with low blood pressure. I turned off the road as soon as possible, and having pushed the front seat right back, reclined it almost to the horizontal. After a while he began to feel better, but as soon as he was nearly upright again, he felt ill. I was beginning to panic by now: 'We'll have to go back. It's not safe with you like this. I'll get back on the motorway in the other direction.' This was completely unacceptable to Gareth. 'I'm going home. Drive on! Just don't take any notice of how I look.' This was easier said than done, but in the end I did drive on with the seat leaning quite far back. It was a miserable journey and I thought we were taking a big risk, but his pleasure on arrival outweighed the discomfort. By this time we had been given a pair of hinged, fibre-glass ramps. They were expensive and very strong, yet I hated them, feeling they were unstable. Anyway, Matthew and I managed to get him in through the front door using these. In spite of the horrors of the journey we had somehow managed to get Gareth from Rookwood into our home without assistance. I tried to think it was another step forward, but if there never was any improvement in his condition, life was clearly going to be far from easy.

We had continued working on our home, preparing it for Gareth's permanent residence ever since his first return a few weeks ago. The builder had promised to treat finishing the shower room as a matter of urgency and it was almost ready. So at last we could get Gareth's bed into what would be our new bedroom. Now that he didn't have to sleep in the study, he started to think about sorting out the complete confusion of books and papers. Of one thing we were all certain – Gareth would have to be involved in the process at every stage. It is true that there were disorganised areas in the old study, such as my desk and the mountains of children's stationery accumulated over the years. But his desk was always scrupulously neat, and he had prided himself on being able to pick out any book from the shelves with ease and locate any file. The present scene filled him with horror, doubly so because he couldn't do the hands-on sorting-out himself. Though, if consulting my own wishes I would have suggested a relaxing weekend, it was obvious we were going to tackle the study. With much of one wall taken up by his desk and another by the piano, it was something of a puzzle to fit in all the bookcases, ranging from the elegant Swedish ones purchased when we first furnished a house, to white wood ones bought at some later date. Where would we start?

We decided that the most awkward fittings should be positioned first, namely our two adjacent teak desks which formed part of a system of shelving, supported by three plastic-coated 'ladders'. Though it was just about free-standing, the tops of each ladder had to be screwed into the wall. Here was one of Gareth's earliest tastes of watching me struggle with what would have been an easy task for him – as if the whole business of the communal organising of his highly personal books and papers wasn't bad enough. First, I had to line up the three ladders exactly and mark with pencil the places for the screws. Matthew helped me hold the whole structure together while Gareth directed. Next I was introduced to the electric drill and the mystery of Rawlplugs. The drill seemed to have a will of its own and the noise it made seemed deafening. I always thought the drill-bit was digging too deeply and kept stopping in alarm. Gareth was stretching his linguistic skills to the utmost in describing how you 'knew' when it was at the right depth. I tried to joke and enjoyed bashing in the plugs, though getting the screws in straight was a harder matter. The desks held up but I could see what it was doing to Gareth to be reduced to the status of foreman.

These all too brief, trial home visits were not just wonderful releases for Gareth from hospital, and for Matthew and me from constant journeys, as well as long days spent in inactivity by his chair or bedside. They also slowly acclimatised us to the new state of things. While we still felt a cure would be possible, we had to work out a way of living with Gareth paralysed from the chest down. He was going to be constantly frustrated to an unthinkable extent by his helplessness and at the same time accept being waited on. At this stage I took on my new role with confidence and zest. I was sure I had the endurance and strength to carry out all the physical activities needed by us both. (It is as well that we had no idea of the almost unendurable strain of different kinds that we would each be under as time went on – and indeed will live with to the end of our days.) As it happened, these weekends were so full of preparation for the great homecoming, and we were so happy in seeing that end draw near, that we noted but didn't dwell on difficulties.

On Friday, 11 December, well over five months after the accident, Gareth was allowed to leave Rookwood. He always says that Dr Grove would not normally let patients in his condition out so soon, but she judged I would be able to cope. (I was pleased with the thought, true or not.) Anyway, she could no longer resist his pleading and we had proved ourselves capable of at least surviving weekends at home. She reminded us that the most common cause for return to hospital was bedsores and warned us to be ever vigilant in skin care. A few kindly nurses had tried to tell us that leaving them was not really an end of our troubles, but the beginning of a very difficult period. Now Dr Grove said, 'You have a tough ten years ahead of you. It takes that time to be reconciled to disability.' Her manner was sad and, clearly, she spoke the truth as she saw it – and intended to give some encouragement also, because the assumption was there would one day be an acceptance of what had happened. Unfortunately there was another assumption behind her words, namely that Gareth would remain paralysed. We still had a vestige of hope for a cure, but listened soberly to this prediction.

The shower room was finished just in time; there was a concrete ramp to the back door; a hospital bed had been delivered; and most of the house was suitably organised. Come what may, Gareth was on his way home. Temporarily we looked no further than this most partial realisation of our wildest dreams. As we drove down the motorway, proving that we did not meditate a quick return by leaving nothing of Gareth's in hospital, that elusive but powerful hope swelled. All the cautious and pessimistic predictions we had heard vanished at a stroke. We thought of that pathetic figure in Intensive Care, unable to breathe, to eat, to speak or even to move a hand. We thought of the gradual transformation to his present state in which he could sit upright in his wheelchair for most of the day, chatter freely without gasping for breath, feed himself and use a typewriter. One more such transformation and what would he be able to do then? If he regained a little voluntary hand movement, that, in time, could be extended to the rest of his body – we might even see him walk again! CRI and Rookwood had done what they could, now it was up to us, his family. This would be our quest which we would approach with the utmost determination and every iota of the boundless energy we felt vibrating in readiness. Without doubt we would succeed. Surely he deserved to get better; he must get better; surely he would . . .

again, he actually could locate and touch his own forehead. On reflection it also showed all he had lost and the infinite number of difficult, if not impossible, tiny gains needed before he could begin to approach any 'normal' activity. Sometimes it was hard to equate the present feeble invalid with the ever-active person of the past.

Again from the third week we were encouraged to watch the physiotherapists practising their other main function, namely massaging the chest until the phlegm was loosened. This was crucial, because only then was a long, thin tube passed through the 'trache' hole into the lungs, and when it was withdrawn there was a thick, yellowish-grey liquid filling a considerable length of it. The used part was thrown away and the process repeated several times until much less of the tube was filled with each insertion. Occasionally it would scrape the side of the windpipe which would get very sore. I was taught how to suction the lungs in this way in case of emergency, but was not at all confident, fearing to damage a lung – the tube did not slide down the windpipe as smoothly or as readily as I had hoped.

Some physiotherapists and nurses were absolutely wonderful at loosening the 'gunge'. Sylvia, though short and slight, was the champion. She would pummel vigorously at the chest with the edges of her upright hands and bring up yards of noxious fluid, to admiring cries from everyone. How Gareth longed to see her on duty in the evening because it meant a restful night for him. Unfortunately not all the nurses were equally skilful at this and he dreaded the appearance of those who lacked the knack of loosening the phlegm, so failing to suction it into the tube. He knew there would be difficulty in breathing until the next physiotherapist visit, usually not before ten o'clock the next morning.

I think it was 20 July when all the family were watching our favourite physiotherapist, John, at work on Gareth. A tall, dark, young man, he was friendly, sympathetic and exceptionally efficient. Above all he would not stick to his time limit (between twenty minutes and half an hour), but stayed until he was sure Gareth's chest was clear. When things were going badly he would pop in when least expected to perform his life-giving 'miracle'. These extra visits were made in his free time. Once, in all seriousness he said, 'there are some chests I just can't keep away from!' We smiled at this, but felt nearer to tears. There spoke the true professional with deep understanding of the patient's suffering and of the difference he could and would make, even at the cost of hours of unpaid work.

Today he joked cheerily as he performed passive exercises with Gareth's legs. Suddenly, when by chance our three pairs of eyes were focussed on Gareth's right foot, it actually moved of its own accord! The whole family was transfixed with joy, at last scenting an end to our troubles. 'John, did you see that. It moved! It moved by itself! He must be getting better!' John avoided our eyes, 'Well, you see, it's not quite like that. Gareth didn't move that foot. It really did move by itself – without him willing it to happen – or even feeling it. It wasn't a voluntary movement, but a muscular spasm.' He looked sadly round our stricken faces. Then as he massaged the chest he told us hesitatingly that in some patients, and he was careful to stress not all, these muscular spasms grew strong and could become a problem. It was so obvious that he did not want to worry us but felt we should begin to be prepared for what in all probability would be a very difficult future, that I was deeply moved by the rich concern which was the defining mark of his nature. At the same time I despaired that these involuntary movements were incompatible with normal action, rather a regular feature of tetraplegia, and hence another step on the downward path.

A few days later John came to tell us he was being transferred to quite another part of the hospital and wouldn't be able to pop in to give extra treatment to those not deemed to be his patients. Gareth was devastated and tried to give adequate thanks for all that had been done. I only hope John was, and is, fully aware of how much he meant to us all.

During this third week the whole family had become habituated to the tense, nerve-wracking atmosphere of IC. Nothing could have been further from the environment I would wish for sensitive young people. It was impossible for them, as anyone else, to spend so many hours in such a ward without getting emotionally involved with other patients and their relatives. Obviously each bed was occupied by someone who was desperately ill. The policy of the nurses and doctors was, 'Where there's life, there's hope' and they worked feverishly on what seemed utterly incurable cases. I think it true to say, though I may be wrong, that very many of the intake died.

On 22 July all three of us were sitting idly in the waiting room ready to be re-admitted to IC. As usual we had been excluded while a new patient was brought in and attached to vital machinery. We had just about finished a hastily procured drink when two deeply distressed ladies were ushered in by a nurse. She left them after a few kind words and I hesitated over whether we should leave too. The younger of the two was saying, 'Mam, he's in the safest place now. He'll be OK. You've got to stop this crying – it won't help Dad if you make yourself ill, will it?' Slowly the older lady calmed down, and perhaps to give her feelings some relief, was soon telling us the full story. Her husband had seemed to be getting over a major heart attack and had been allowed to leave hospital. Early today he had lost consciousness and was rushed here by ambulance. Already they had been told that several of his organs were in a state of collapse and to expect the worst. No wonder they were upset! What could we say for comfort, except refer to the dedication of the staff, especially Dr Franklin? Over the next three or four days he hovered between life and death. The ladies moved into 'Arosfa' to save a long daily journey 'down the valley'. Regularly we shared the agonies of this family, hearing such details as made us regretfully think that it might be kinder all round to let him die in peace. But we were proved wrong and the ward policy completely justified when the man, before Gareth left IC, had sufficiently recovered to be transferred to his local hospital.

Not so very long after, I came into the ward one morning to see a young man I had not seen before occupying a corner bed. Only his head was visible and it was heavily bandaged. He lay absolutely still and what were probably grieving parents sat at his side. Somehow the atmosphere was particularly grim and Sylvia, who happened to be on duty, whispered, 'That boy was joy-riding on a stolen motorbike last night. There was a gang of them speeding at random round the city. He crashed and got brain damaged. There's no hope. His brain is swelling and nothing in the world will stop it.' She was near to tears, stunned by this pointless tragedy. And he did die some hours later. There was no noise, he just stopped breathing. Again we were asked to wait outside and were amazed to see that the corridor and stairs leading to the ward were lined on both sides with many leather-clad youths consoling themselves with beer or stronger drinks. It was a strange experience, threading our way between these ranks, and they caused some alarm to the hospital staff, but they were silent and stricken with grief. (They did, however, fill the chairs in the waiting room while elderly visitors stood, and left a mess of cans, bottles and crisp packets behind.) They were allowed, a few at a time, into the ward to bid farewell to their friend and I have never seen a more genuine sense of loss. We were struck with the tragic waste of this young life, but almost equally saddened to be told by one pleasantly spoken and sad friend of the dead man that they would be joy-riding again that night.

Without doubt it was the young patients whose plight saddened everyone the most. Only days later another victim of a traffic accident was carried in. He was a good-looking, muscular young man who had been driving his younger sister to school to help his parents. The girl was taken to a local hospital, but he, being more seriously injured, was rushed to CRI. At first he seemed to be paralysed, but to everyone's joy, he began to move his limbs, first slowly and then with vigour. Indeed it became a problem to keep him in bed as he struggled with all his might to get out. The nurses laughed as they wrestled with him, but it was a serious matter stopping him damaging his 'lines'. Soon we wondered why the parents' happiness quickly evaporated – then a nurse told us his injury was to the head and it looked as if he was brain-damaged. Investigations were going on to find the extent of this, but as in Gareth's case, nothing could be finally established until the swelling went down. At least he would live. I spoke at length several times daily with the worried parents and soon I felt close to them as we huddled together in the Maskrey waiting room. They proudly described their son as being in the peak of physical condition, a hard worker and seemingly possessed of every virtue. 'Why should it happen to someone like him?' they kept on asking. Like us, they found it difficult to come to terms with unmerited disaster. Before he was transferred to another hospital he seemed to recognise his parents and say his name, but that was all. We never found out if he got better, though his father had promised to let us know. Assuming his son recovered, and as a way of thanking the hospital staff, he planned to visit the hospital regularly, helping in any way he could. However Gareth was moved to another ward eventually, so we may have missed him if he did come. But I have an awful feeling that the boy stayed brain damaged.

For almost three weeks Gareth was in IC. Whatever his specific condition, death was never far away in that ward. Once or twice we saw the emergency procedure for cardiac arrest. Sometimes we were aware of unusually hectic activity around a patient's bed. At least three times after noticing this we were speedily sent to the waiting room and the door firmly shut. This only happened after someone had died and we would listen for the sounds of the covered bed being wheeled away. Then occasionally the relatives of the deceased would come in and we offered what comfort we could. Usually one of the three main doctors from IC would also come to talk about what had happened and offer sympathy. Sometimes, familiar people would just vanish from the waiting room and we could only assume that the worst had happened for them. The atmosphere was depressing and exhausting, yet most of the relatives and friends were able to sympathise with each other.

If it was terrible for the visitors, what of the staff? Gradually we were getting to know some quite well and learnt how they felt about their demanding work. It seemed that the IC nurses, though seemingly coping with everything, even cardiac arrests, in a matter of fact, positive way could find their jobs very depressing, especially if a series of patients designated to their particular care died. Sometimes they felt as if they were achieving nothing. Once the more fortunate patients began to mend they were moved to other wards or hospitals, so the nurses seldom saw a healthy product of their efforts. On one occasion I thought a particularly friendly and committed nurse was looking decidedly unwell. She explained how she had spent the whole of the previous day sponging blood as it welled out of her patient. I remembered him; his wife had told me all about the massive operation he had seemed to survive so well. But early the following morning he had started to bleed and, though the specialists struggled for hours, it could not be stopped. That night the nurse had vivid nightmares in which she continued to wipe the blood from the dying man. When she got into work his bed was empty. You had to be hardened to survive she said, but sometimes 'it got to you'.

It is quite obvious that Bethan and Matthew had lived through some terrible experiences, not only to do with Gareth. They took it in turns to be in the ward and there was no hiding from them the awful things that were happening all around. Once we insisted they had lunch in town and, in general, tried to encourage them to continue with their own activities where possible. Now we had to insist that Matthew did not miss his National Youth Orchestra course. From the time Bethan was thirteen, one or other, and sometimes both, had played in this orchestra. It was a tremendous honour to be chosen out of young musicians throughout Great Britain. There were three courses a year, one in each of the main school holidays, but in the summer the final concert was a 'Prom' in the Royal Albert Hall in London and this was always the most thrilling experience. Bethan had just reached the retirement age and so, sadly, could no longer play, but Matthew had been looking forward to this NYO course and the National Chamber Orchestra tour which followed. Gareth was absolutely determined he was not going to miss out on these unique opportunities and, at last, won the day. My problem was how to sort out clothes for Matthew, because he had been in Villiers Park for a week and another ten days in hospital where we could only wash underclothes and drape them round our room to dry. Bethan again offered to look after her father and we decided to go on Wednesday the 27th, in the afternoon and return early the next morning. I could wash, dry and iron clothes for the three of us in that time.

I was loth to leave her, remembering the two awful occasions when Gareth was so ill. At least this time he was in IC and Bethan would not stay in the ward at night. Besides, his condition was stable now, as the consultant assured us. Anyway we went and got all the packing done in record time. It was heart warming to see that neighbours two doors away had cut the lawn and hedge, even weeded the path. We caught an early train back. As we waited for entry into the ward, a nurse informed us that Gareth had been moved back to Thomas Andrew ward half an hour previously! An accident victim in a desperate condition needed a bed and, since he was the fittest of the patients at the time, he was chosen to move.

How happy I was that Bethan had not suffered agonies over this change. She knew her father was so much better, at least in respect of his breathing and also that he had gained a little strength. It was wonderful for the three of us to realise that his condition was not considered dangerous any more – so that the move seemed almost to be a 'good thing'. It was also a relief to move freely in and out of the ward without waiting to slip in unobtrusively. But as time elapsed we began to get more and more subdued. He was now in a ward which contained, I believe, more than twenty patients. On duty at any one time were a sister, an auxiliary and a student. How on earth could Gareth get the close observation he needed? He was unable to speak to attract attention and his arm movements were feeble. Suppose he urgently needed help? Eventually we hit upon a solution: if he could push off the oxygen monitor that was clipped to his finger, the alarm would sound and the nurses would come.

Bethan left to stay the night with friends in Bristol, so Matthew and I sat trying to keep Gareth entertained with one eye on the screen which displayed the level of oxygen getting through to his blood-stream. A few times this began to drop, but deeper breathing for a little while cleared the tubes and the level rose again. Two good 'physio' sessions helped tremendously. Quite late in the evening Gareth started to struggle to draw breath and the pulse-oxymeter reading plummeted. I encouraged him to take several deep breaths, but this time the levels continued to drop. Then I made a worrying discovery, namely that the alarm was not working. It should have sounded long before. Because we had been watching the levels so carefully, there had been no time for the alarm to be activated before he had taken evasive action – otherwise we would have spotted this problem earlier. I called the sister who tried to reassure us, saying that she would watch the machine all night. I knew this to be impossible, especially since Gareth's bed was nowhere near the cubicle where the nurses sat. The oxygen intake was already dangerously low and who knew when emergency action would be needed? My heart sank – I would have to impose my will, this time in earnest, once again. Feeling very shaky and mindful of my 'lecture' in Intensive Care, I was exquisitely polite but absolutely determined: 'If it's alright with you, to set my mind at rest I would like to stay all night in the ward with Gareth. Bethan and I always took it in turns throughout the night when he was in Thomas Andrew ward previously. Matthew is here to share the watch with me now, so we'll be fine. We've had lots of sleep recently. We can keep an eye on the level for you.' The whole thing was upsetting, but what else could I do? If the alarm didn't sound, Gareth could deteriorate rapidly. The nurse looked bemused: 'Honestly, I personally will watch him all the time. You need a rest.' I insisted, 'Really, it's no problem for us. We'll stay.' The discussion continued, until recognising my determination, the sister rather resentfully got someone from IC to set the machine properly – it was in perfect working order. I was grateful and extraordinarily relieved. As it was very late by now, Matthew and I reluctantly agreed to rest for a couple of hours. However, I was by no means convinced that Gareth would have adequate supervision in that crowded ward and slept badly. At least with this example of my 'interference' there seemed to be no residual ill-will.

As it happened Gareth survived the night reasonably well, with the machine not alarming very often and, in the daylight, we forgot the worries of the previous evening. Then there was a pleasant surprise in the afternoon; Gareth was given a different kind of 'trache', again with a speaking tube which, hopefully, would be more successful than the last. Gareth was thrilled to have his voice back and become one tiny degree nearer his usual talkative self. Unfortunately his oxygen mask did not work very well, since the elastic which was supposed to clamp it tightly round his face had to stretch round the traction apparatus as well and left gaps. Insufficient oxygen was reaching his lungs and, in any case, the pressure made him panic. Then, a day or two later, this mask was replaced by a nose-tube and, though it delivered less oxygen, it was more comfortable. A suitable collar was found to replace the traction, but this rubbed Gareth's skin mercilessly and we stuffed its edges with cotton wool, so he had a crazy, Father Christmas look.

In spite of all these problems the days passed more cheerfully than might be expected. Gareth was able to chat to his usual procession of visitors; indeed he would become animated and responsive. It is true that his appetite was slight and varied, also his temperature tended to rise and there was a constant battle to keep the chest clear. The medical highlights of each day were the visits of the 'physios', especially the last one, which determined the quality of his night. Everyone feared another chest infection but, temporarily at least, he seemed to be fighting them off.

Never forgotten was the terrible suspense about whether the paralysis would remain. Each passing day of no improvement in movement or feeling meant a slight increase in the probability of this state continuing permanently. Gareth pestered the experts for information and especially for predictions, which were not forthcoming. Visitors brought encouraging stories which gave momentary hope. This big, all-consuming terror was underlying all the other lesser, yet important, hopes and fears concerning his condition. At least for the most part we no longer thought he was going to die. Unfortunately this was to change in the all-too-near future.

Interlude

Journey to Aberystwyth (1992)

Towards midnight a car, with poor visibility, crawled through dense mist and steady, wetting drizzle to the parking space nearest to the door of a block of flats. A fairly smartly dressed woman hastily lifted out, then assembled, a 'push-along' wheelchair, next positioning it very precisely in the small space between the passenger door and the front seat. Reaching for a sliding board, she pushed it gently but firmly under the disabled man and tried to ease him across to the chair. A dead weight, he slumped against the gear lever and, in spite of increasingly feverish attempts, could not be moved. There was no one about, the flats were in total darkness, the damp air invaded the fragile lungs and the rain drifted relentlessly into the car . . .

I woke with a strange air of unreality. Then in a flash I remembered that I was sleeping downstairs in a single bed and that Gareth was at home with me, only two yards away. He had been in hospital for well over five months and yesterday had been discharged. As if this were not sufficiently momentous, we were about to embark on a foolhardy expedition to Aberystwyth. Today was the centenary of the University's Education Department, and there was to be a celebratory dinner including the presentation of a volume of the newly-published history of the department (called *Fit to Educate*) to Gareth. He had told the organiser there was an outside possibility that he would get there, but not to expect him. It was sad to see his state of mind, which compounded a deep longing to be there with a rational assessment of the dangers of such an expedition. I was fully committed to making the journey, thinking it would be a tremendous psychological boost for him to be among his colleagues once more, thus preserving a hope that one day he could take up his professional role again. I also had the strongest possible support for this plan from our friends Margaret and James who were at the scene of the accident, and together we had persuaded the dubious Gareth at least to make an effort to be present.

It had already been arranged that a district nurse would come every morning to get Gareth up. Before she arrived this morning, to my horror, I noticed that there was no urine in the night bag. We realised that the catheter must be blocked. This was an emergency, since the urine would build up in the bladder and cause serious problems. In some ways an in-dwelling catheter was easy to manage, because normally it didn't need to be changed so it was just a case of keeping an eye on the unobtrusive leg-bag and emptying it when necessary. However once in hospital it had somehow got pulled out accidentally, with considerable bleeding, and replacing it, we learnt, was something that required special training which, obviously, I didn't have. Tetraplegics are prone to bladder infections and, I think, some kind of deposit or lining is formed which peels away and blocks the tubes. This had happened several times and, apart from antibiotics, special bladder washes are used which, however, caused different problems later. When, on this particular morning, we told the nurse what had happened, she said that only one nurse in our district could do the job and she wasn't on duty. This was a sad blow to our hopes for the day, but also, more significantly, a very real and immediate danger for Gareth. There was much phoning between different nurses and eventually the only one who could help was tracked down, helping in some charitable concern. To her infinite credit, and our infinite relief, she rushed over in her smart attire to sort out the problem.

As the original district nurse carried on washing and dressing Gareth, I reflected that the same thing would be unlikely to recur in the near future and pressed on with the packing. I did know that there were other difficulties, however. At this stage Gareth's blood pressure was still unstable so that at any moment he could begin to feel light-headed and his vision break up. (He couldn't be left on his own, even for short periods, and until a friend lent me a baby alarm, a five-minute bath was a tense experience and as likely as not I would run up and down stairs a few times, dripping!) I knew well enough by now how to cope with these pressure drops by tipping the wheelchair back until it was almost horizontal and holding it there until he recovered. He was also allowed a limited number of ephedrine tablets which would raise the pressure after about twenty minutes of discomfort. The question was whether he could sit upright through a longish ceremony and the dinner, especially since any food caused his blood pressure to plummet. I was a little more confident about the journey, however, having already discovered that it was possible to tilt the front seat of the car sufficiently far back to effect a recovery. If he did actually faint, which he had never done yet, I wouldn't know what to do, a thought which I must admit was somewhat unnerving.

Gareth's chest at this time seemed to be free from infection and he hadn't needed phlegm to be suctioned through the 'trache' hole for several weeks. Indeed this hole was supposed to be closing up naturally, but was very slow to do so – and it had to be cleaned and dressed daily. If the lungs did suddenly become congested, we would have to seek medical help immediately. We had no idea of the telephone number of a doctor in Aberystwyth and had made no contingency plans in the case of disaster, apart from thinking we would rouse a kind neighbour and ask him to get help. This showed an astonishing lack of forethought on our part, rather than confidence that all would be well.

One final problem was of quite a different sort: namely, driving past the place of the accident. Surprisingly, Gareth had got used to being driven in a car (and by me!) without too much trauma, but actually to re-live the moment of seeing that other car skidding towards him at speed must be deeply upsetting. We discussed other routes, but since this was the quickest he decided to confront the challenge now. On later journeys, as we passed the spot, we have both unintentionally referred to it as 'where we died' – interesting for the 'we' as well as 'died' – and not as histrionic as it seems at first.

Gone were the days of travelling light or easily. It had become and remains a planned exercise. I had packed a huge quantity of medical equipment, including a Spenco mattress, and very few clothes. We had made a check-list of the most important things, but it's always a worry that